in that stillness...

BY THE SAME AUTHOR:

Looking at Life

in that stillness...

A JOURNAL OF
ONGOING EXPLORATIONS
1978–1979

DANIEL CASTRO

Journey Publications
WOODSTOCK, NEW YORK

IN THAT STILLNESS . . .
COPYRIGHT © 1980 BY DANIEL CASTRO

All rights reserved, including the right to reproduce this book, or parts thereof, in any form, except for the inclusion of brief quotations in a review.

First Printing, April 1980
Published by Journey Publications
   PO Box 423, Woodstock, NY 12498
Text type (ten point Sabon) set by
   New Hampshire Composition, Concord, NH
Cover printed by Profile Press, New York, NY
Book printed and bound by Braun-Brumfield, Inc., Ann Arbor, MI

Library of Congress Catalog Card # 79-92054
ISBN: 0-918038-12-x

Printed in the United States of America.

Dedication

In June of 1972, I met Dr. R. P. Kaushik — and in that I discovered the true nature of aloneness.

Namasté —

To a loving teacher and friend.

PUBLISHER'S NOTE

During the summers of 1978 and 1979, Daniel Castro held a series of talks, retreats, and discussions in Ithaca, Montreal, and Woodstock. The Woodstock retreat was an especially intense time, during which twenty to twenty-five people lived and worked closely together throughout the summer. This allowed a deep exploration to take place, in which the discoveries made were actually applied in day-to-day living.
in that stillness . . . is a record of what took place during that time. The reader is invited to participate in that intensity and feeling of affection.

Woodstock, New York
December 1979

Contents

I. TALKS

    The Journey Within Silence   3
    The Important Question   7
    The Need for Essence   24
    A Life in Freedom   29
    A Love That is True   35
    The Face of Love   38
    Passages   45

II. DISCUSSIONS AND DEEPER ENQUIRIES

    Introduction   75
    The Responsibility of Communication   76
    The Communication of Freedom   84
    The Essential Relationship   89
    The Language of Silence   100
    A Deepening Yearning   105
    The Response to a Human Being   111
    The Qualities of Resistance   116
    Coming to the Point of Stillness   120
    The Flowering of a Human Heart   126
    Seeing the Ocean   131
    No Other Life   135
    A Life Beyond Hurt   145
    The Child of Intelligence   149
    The Social Issue   158
    One Need in Life   163
    When the Heart Speaks   170
    Passages   177

III. REFLECTIONS

    From the Author's Journal   197

I. TALKS

The Journey Within Silence

Questioner: How do I gain that quality of energy, bring that quality of energy into my life?

Daniel: This question is often posed — how to bring this energy into everyday life? How to bring this silence or essence, or love into our everyday existence? I think we've all experienced it. In fact, in this room we may experience a meditative quality, and yet our day may be quite chaotic and confused. So it seems to me it's a collective question. It may come from you, but I've heard it in the last few weeks here in different ways. Does everyone understand the question — how to bring quality, how to bring a dynamic quality into our everyday life — or, is that dynamic quality only reserved for certain times, certain occasions?

The first thing I must state is that this energy or this silence is not something personal. So the first understanding is that you cannot bring this energy. In fact, the full impact of this energy is the absence of you — your plans, your desires, your ideas. It cannot be used. It's pure. You can't do anything with it. But you make the discovery that without it life has no meaning; and all the activity, all the human activity, all the gestures, all the attempts, have no meaning without this understanding. And yet it has no power, it has no name.

So all one's plans, all one's attempts are washed away when one feels this silence. That's an important thing to understand. It's simply not personal. When I understand the limitations of the attempt to expand myself through the accumulation of knowledge or objects, when I understand the futility of my projection and the accumulation, I have come to the end of everything I know. I don't know anything more than that. I see that salvation is not in my having a large accumulation of power or money; I see in fact that the money and the accumulation of power become a burden in my life, they don't enhance it. And I also now see the limitation of joining an organization, or a club, or acquiring a philosophy — I see that's also an attempt to expand myself, through identification. Now I become an American, or a Canadian, or an existentialist, or whatever — a Communist, or a Christian, or a Buddhist, or a Hindu. I've tried to expand my field. When I see an inherent limitation in that also — whatever I accumulate, I'm still no more than what I am, and whatever philosophy or religion I arm myself with, I still equal me — when I see I cannot be more than I am, then I start to examine this 'me'.

Solely and purely, life is now an examination of the nature of 'me'. That's meditation, that's my enquiry, that is my whole need to understand. And I focus my attention on it. I see my reactions, I'm aware of my responses, I'm aware of the effect I create in the society around me. I see when buttons are pushed in me and how I react, and I see how I create reactions in others. And slowly I start to understand its workings. When I examine my identity with such an intensity, such a sharpness and interest, I am introduced to layer upon layer; to its workings, to its silence. I'm seeing how it works, I'm seeing how it's put together. And when I enquire into it, I'm introduced to all human history. When I look at myself with such intensity, I understand why the whole human race has evolved the way it has. I understand the nature of the whole construct of human history. When I look at myself, I see all of time, from the beginning, and I see all the hopes for the future.

At that point I'm introduced to myself as the human race. And still the answer isn't there; and still I go deeper. The reason I'm going deeper now is because there's still a yearning. Whatever I've discovered — now that I see what I am, what collectively we are, and I see the whole human condition, the whole human history — still the answer is not there. I've seen more than I did a week ago, or a year ago, but it's still not the answer — and I yearn to understand the answer. That yearning takes me even deeper.

Is it clear so far? Because I'm not talking about something uncommon or unusual, or something you have to be heroic, or an amazing human being to do. I'm talking about something that a common human being can do — someone with an average mind, someone with a simple background. It's the average person who can see that there's some lack, that there's some great need, and this average person has the opportunity to enquire.

Now you come to a point in the enquiry where it is your whole life. It is no longer something you do under stress. It is no longer something you just do when you're in pain or sorrow. But you come to a point in the enquiry where there is absolutely nothing else for you to do but to look, to feel, to understand. That's how deep the yearning goes. And this yearning, when it comes to this point, is no longer simple yearning — it is a passion. Every cell in your body is united now; there is a total movement. There's a passion to understand, a passion to feel, a passion to experience. And you find that whatever you've discovered so far serves as an introduction to further discovery.

When you come to this point in your life that we can call passion — not a passion to accumulate anything more, but that life is simply passion for you — then the response to that passion is now essence. This passion is seeing the essence of things, and when that passion is great enough, it will not accept a limited answer. The need is to see the essence of things, and the response to that passion is essence. When the essence and the passion meet, when a human being and God meet, when a male and a female meet in that passion, in that intensity, a vital quality is born; creativity has taken place. The quality that comes out of that passion and essence, that male and female, that human being and God, is stillness.

When you come to this point of stillness, every heartbeat, every breath, every sound, every sight takes you deeper. The very common things that you've done all your life, that were boring to you, that had no meaning to you — your simple daily life, by its very nature, is now taking you deeper. Every breath takes you deeper, every sound you hear takes you deeper, everything you see takes you deeper. You've come to a journey without end. Until you touch that quality in your life, every activity will be limited. And when you approach this point, you start to understand that without that, there's no life. Without that, I've just been going through the motions. Without that, it's just empty. All my heartache, all my ideas, all my conflict, all my pressures, all my torment, have nothing to do with life. The actual meditation is eating, sleeping, breathing, heartbeat, sound — that's the meditation. Meditation is life. But now life is a dynamic. It is not a personal existence, and yet you don't need any notion of a collective group or community to support you. When you touch that stillness fully and thoroughly, life is expressed through you. Any expression you have before that merger will not be a full expression at all; it will be limited.

16 July 1979

The Important Question

To be alive is a question — and there is a deep yearning for the answer. And when one realizes that yearning, when one realizes the need, the question that comes out of that realization is a deep energy, is an intense energy. Inherent in that question is the answer or response. When the question is meditated upon, refined, developed, and brought forth, it is no longer a question of seeking information; it embodies a yearning. And if the question is a passion, then the response is an essence. If the question is put with intensity, the answer must be forthcoming. The very form, the very body is a question, your very presence here is a question — and not only presence in this home — but the very fact that you're alive is a question, and it seeks an answer.

In every moment there is an opportunity for a full realization. A full realization doesn't mean that you conclude and stop there, but full realization means that there is no longer an impediment to your journey, you're no longer stuck, you're no longer fixed in a state of conflict, there's no longer a backward pull. Please understand your responsibility — not only in this room, but in this life also. Without the understanding of the simple need, we are destined to repeat the past. We are the extension of the past — the immediate past, and the long-term past of thousands of years; all human history, all human knowledge directs our activity. Without full understanding, life is not free, it is not full. That's why I say that the question is important. The question doesn't only revolve around the issue expressed; the real issue is one of freedom, and the capacity to realize that freedom, and go even deeper than freedom. The question that is meditated upon, that is formulated, that is charged, also creates the receptivity. Receptivity is the key. A pure question is a conservation of energy.

I come to a point in life where I yearn — not for anything, because I understand the limitation in anything I can acquire. But still the need is there. The very yearning that I experience, the very need that I experience, indicates that the possibility exists; I wouldn't experience the need without the possibility. But I don't know a way. So I'm no longer yearning *for*. I just am living in a state of need — and it's a need beyond anything I know.

Now, someone brought up the question today, what happens in one's life when one realizes that what one called love, what one called affection, what one called relationship, one realizes has never been love. I may have believed in it as I was doing it, but now, in retrospect, the shattered experience indicates to me that it was really a mediocre affair; it was a clinging, a fear of loss, a holding on, stimulation, depression. So I see at one point — or I'm about to see at one point — that I've never loved at all; in one's own words, not that someone is feeding it to you, but you've experienced that. Before you experience that totally, there will be a great pressure not to. You'll experience what you call fear — fear of making that discovery totally and completely. Because the discovery that you don't know what love is, is actually the ending of the known. And the known struggles to survive. The known generates fear as a means of survival.

So the full recognition that you don't know what love is, you don't know what life is — really — the full recognition of that *is* the receptivity. Because at that point you no longer have the reference point to the known; you're no longer defining what is happening to you. You are no longer imposing your condition on life around you and inside of you; you don't know. When you don't know what love is, and you yearn, that yearning is the receptivity necessary to the experience.

Now you may experience what I could call stillness — just a stillness. Last evening I mentioned this in conjunction with an afterglow that sometimes takes place after a sexual experience — when both parties have exhausted themselves, and there's a quality where you desire nothing, you're finished; and you can melt

The Important Question   9

into each other, or you can be alone, or whatever, you want nothing more. The only thing is, that state comes only after exhaustion; whereas to me that would be the primary state — not the state that you arrive at, but the state that you start with. The non-desire state would be the basis of lovemaking. Because the very fact of desiring is the separation. You cannot desire what you are, you only desire what is out there. So this attempt to incorporate 'out there', by its very nature, is separation. To close that gap, you must perform, you must seduce, you must parade, you must do so many things. When you have that indication of desire, that will be your first signal to be careful.

Questioner: At times I experience that stillness, but then I lose it.

Daniel: That feeling of loss indicates that what I experienced before is not enough. It doesn't invalidate the experience. But we tend to make a habit of the experience and want to repeat it. So that it's not taking place is your invitation to go deeper. In its absence, I yearn. And when I yearn in that way, there's no absence as such. I'm introduced to another dimension of this energy. And I'll find again, a moment later, that it's still not enough. What I can see happening is that there's a mutation taking place, a transformation. The very cellular structure is changing; there's a readiness. What you were trying to attain all your life is taking place, but now you're discovering that each time you feel it, it's not enough — it's an introduction to going deeper. You cannot volunteer that state, and you can't fake it, and you can't invent it; it's just a fact. Once you've established an ego center called 'me', then this center called 'me' tends to possess. And the first possession is that it claims your body as its own, and with that it tends and attempts to get feedback, to accumulate more and more — to build around itself. So obviously when you discover a life beyond the center called 'me', you've also discovered the ending of ownership. Life can't be owned. So when you experience the absence, don't run from it, don't try to change it; yearn a bit more now.

Q: *But when disturbances start coming up, these feelings or* thoughts, and you see that they're still there — even though you know in your heart that's not what you want, that you want something more, you want to be free — where is it coming from, and what do you do with it?

Daniel: Why are you required to do anything with it?

Q: But it disturbs me.

Daniel: What's the nature of these disturbances? I don't doubt that they come up. At one point, any time you even approach clarification, everything that you've experienced in life may come to the surface; the whole human experience may come to the surface through time. You may experience not only what you know to be so in your own life, your own personal experience; you may experience the whole knowledge and information and history of the human race, in one way or another. Before recognition can take place, you'll have to go through the whole structure, the whole pressure of the conditioning; you'll have to see it first-hand. The reason that these things come to the surface is that a purification is taking place. So there will be subtle pressures and conditions; you'll be called, you'll be pulled. But I don't know why you have the idea that you must do something when they come. That's the trap. So then understand that the doer is there. Because this energy of stillness, the quality of stillness I'm talking about, is not a doer. Stillness is the capacity to wait — because we're talking about a love that waits. Stillness is the need in the human being, because what is also taking place, in this energy called God, is waiting. Stillness is the capacity, the first step in recognition. So, when you say that you yearn for God, or you need something deeper than that, it may not be a full enough realization of that need.

Questioner: Is it just by seeing this stillness, that mutation of the self starts happening? What point do you have to come to before the ego starts dissolving?

Daniel: When you see how it works, you see the whole structure of projection. Any attempt to cut across your own projection just furthers it, and makes it more clever. You see that the duplicity of mind as a survival instrument is enormous — as quickly as you see something it's able to incorporate it. What I am doing is surviving — by incorporating, by owning, by possessing. And essentially, I always come up short. I find through my possessions of all these beautiful things, that when I own them, they cease to be beautiful.

Michael: Why does the intimacy with creation appear to be intensity — always?

Daniel: Because there's always a need to move to the source. Each time that you're no longer imposing a condition on yourself, each time that you're no longer living in self-torment or pursuit, the very waiting is a movement to the source. In everything, inherent in everything, you'll see that there's a constant movement to the source. Yet at the same time, psychologically, there's always a movement away, to create your own center.

M: So this stillness isn't stillness as we know it.

Daniel: I have used the word yearning, because to me it seems to be a word that embodies or indicates a fact. Yearning is the attraction. Attraction is not something that you do, attraction is something that you experience, something that exerts a great pull. When in fact you are what you look for, when you are also of the same quality as the love or the God you look for, at that point there's a mutual attraction. If love waits, or God waits, and you wait, then that waiting indicates that there's a certain frequency that you're both on; the qualities are on the same frequency. It's that frequency that brings the merger, not effort. So, what appeared to be an effort towards, was actually the very thing that created the separation. Because only self knows the effort, only a center knows effort.

So what we have called 'doing' in our lives is actually a movement that has no doing at all in it. What we usually call doing is an activity that comes out of anxiety or fear of boredom. This doing in fact is scattered activity. And this doing is fraught with fear; it has nothing to do with reality. To me, full health would be a major discovery in life — that you are no longer the source of friction, that you are not making yourself sick any longer — not that you're moving towards health, not that you're moving towards developing yourself, but that you're no longer creating any more contradictions in your body, that you're no longer tormenting yourself with your thought process. And that is not something that you can develop or achieve or acquire, because the very achievement-orientation is the conflict.

Questioner: *What happens when you discover the self-perpetuation — that you're constantly trying to fill that feeling of lack; and you also discover that all you've done, in all your motivations, was everything else but love, and in fact just perpetuated the movement of that very lack. For some reason I see them being very intertwined right now. What kind of movement takes place once you fully feel that experience — what comes then, what's the unfoldment after that?*

Daniel: You experience that whatever you have done is not true — you truly experience that — and you see there's an emptiness, and an attempt to fill up that emptiness with objects or things or ideas or notions. And it hasn't worked. Moving from the emptiness in fact has increased it, it doesn't seem to have diminished it. So now I can't fill this lack; as soon as I felt a boredom, an emptiness, immediately I would go to a movie, or eat something, or watch TV, or go out, or talk, or meditate — I wanted to do all these things as soon as I felt any pressure. And now I see that almost every activity that I engage in comes out of that. And I'm experiencing that — I'm not shaken by it, I'm not frightened by it; I see it. Now what happens?

Q: *I feel very free.*

Daniel: Then? My energies are no longer going into the activity.

The Important Question 13

All my energies in life went into the pursuit, the activity, I was dissipating my energies. At that point I realize that I can't acquire it. When I realize that, I am now conserving my energies — not that I am holding on to the energies, but I'm no longer running after anything. The need is still there, but I'm no longer pursuing anything, I don't have 'anything' to go after. What does it actually mean to conserve your energy — not in terms of any idea — but to actually experience first-hand the conservation of energy with the understanding that there's nothing to go after?

Q: The highest form that I can experience presently is a feeling of freedom.

Daniel: Okay. I experience not the name of freedom, but the fact of freedom. I experience the cutting of the thread that connects the past to the future — because obviously the pursuit of anything only came out of the past. The past is where I accumulated the identification, and that identification was necessary to run after the goal. So I am no longer connected to the past and the future in the same way.

There is a link in time and continuity from the past to the future. The past is the known, the accumulated information, and this is what I project into the future as a goal. In other words, I project into the future the known, and I tend to repeat the past through that projection. Can I see that I'm living in a cycle of events? Can I understand that this past, as a projection, cannot supply me with fullness, that the projection doesn't have fullness in it?

So when 'this' and 'that' are one movement, there is no longer time and space; I'm no longer a prisoner of time and space, there's no separation in me. This separation was a dissipation of energy. The coming together is now the conservation of energy. I wait. Waiting is a quality of yearning — yearning having the same essential need, but without anything to run after or anything to believe in. When I actually experience this conservation of energy, I'm sharp, I'm vital, and I'm looking, I'm aware — I'm examining any movement, any thought. That intensity, that sharpness will be the introduction further into that stillness. Because that sharpness is now looking at things with such an intensity that the life has transformed. And it, the instrument itself, has changed.

Michael: Then what happens to time?

Daniel: Time, then, is seen to be what it is. It's an agreement. In other words, there's no longer a hope through time; there's no longer a dreamer or a schemer or a planner through time in the same way.

You see the need; and the waiting is the manifestation of that need. I come to a point in life where I see the need for human order, for peace — and I wait for it to take place. And if it is not taking place, then I realize that I haven't fully seen the need, and I go deeper into that need. So at this point I'm experiencing the need for peace in my life, and I'm feeling what I would call a peace in my life — and I also see the effect in the situation around me; I can see the quality of peace around me. And then when there's a disturbance in the community, then I see a greater need for peace in my life, and I go deeper into that. And again, when I see that there's still a disturbance in the world community, then again I see the need to go even deeper.

So when one comes to any point of realization, the realization connects one to all of life. But it's not that one comes to that point and can then dictate what form it will take. You come to that point and you realize that the full realization only takes place in relationship. But relationship is not something you invent or put together; relationship is a response to your intensity. The response to your intensity will be the introduction of that energy to a larger community. Your need is to go deeper. And surrender is necessary to actually see, because without that seeing you're going to attempt to *do*. Seeing the pain or the sorrow of humankind does not equal doing; to see the pain and the sorrow equals feeling. That feeling is the vehicle. And if in fact there's still lack around you, it indicates that the feeling — however intense it is, however sensitive it is — is still not enough.

The Important Question   15

In everything you're doing you're seeing the connection. When life is not your personal property, then you see it as life. Now I may experience life not as personal property, but as life; but I live in a world where people think of life as their personal property. And I see that if you think that life is your personal property, you must live a life of sorrow. So, I see that humankind must live a life of sorrow. There is no way out of it — when life is personal to you, you're going to know all the effects, all the pressures of a personal existence. If you think that you're a man, if you think that you're a woman, if you think that you're black, if you think that you're a German or a Jew — you're going to know the historical or societal pressures inherent in that personal structure; you will feel the burden. And even the reaction to it furthers the burden, because that's proof that you are it. If you didn't think you were it, you wouldn't react to it. So there is no way out — as long as you have a personal structure in any way, shape or form, you are compelled to experience sorrow and pain. So the human condition is sorrow and pain.

Now you come to a point where you're free, and you're living in a world structure of sorrow and pain, and you also see you're helpless in it. You experience something yourself, you see that humanity is you, you are connected to it. When you've experienced freedom yourself, and you see that pain exists in humankind, you experience compassion. That compassion, or that connection — that feeling, that deep feeling — introduces you deeper. That compassion introduces you to a way. When you have touched that quality of compassion, you are able to experience and see a quality of energy in each being. That is relationship. Relationship is when you come to a point in life when you can actually experience and perceive directly the quality of energy in each being. When you focus this quality of perception on anything, light is shed upon it; it reveals itself. And it reveals itself not as something separate. The viewer must understand his connection. If he doesn't understand the connection, he's going to react to what he sees. That is why it has always been said that the face of God will destroy you. To see that is a terrible sight if *you* still exist. To see what is happening is more than you can bear if *you* exist.

Questioner: Recognizing the limitation of the form — and that anything that will come from the form will also manifest as a limitation itself — that recognition goes into another transformation which is compassion. Because there is helplessness there; it's as far as one can go with it.

Daniel: No — form is only limited because you haven't seen it. When you see it, then you're also introduced to a great need, a further need. Because now I'm talking about the possible ending of illness, or not needing exercise to maintain your health. The day before you needed a fixed exercise program, and it was necessary. Now you're introduced to something else — it is no longer exercise, but actually joy in movement. Now you're not rebelling against the form, you're understanding. And when you're understanding, the body is meeting your understanding. The body is responding to your capacity to understand. I'm talking about simple, everyday life now; I'm saying that the dynamic is taking place in the simplicity, in the common. The whole universe is moving in the common activity of the day. And you're able to live according to a schedule, or put the schedule aside; you're not a prisoner of anything, you're moving in it. At that point you're no longer in violation of anything in life. Because if in fact you're only free because you do this, or don't do that, it's still not freedom; it's still an imposed condition. So you are introduced to the need for full freedom, and yet you also understand each time you feel full freedom that there's even deeper to go. So there is no limitation, except the limitation we impose upon ourselves.

Questioner: Then freedom would be a myth?

Daniel: Freedom is only a myth when you try to sustain it.

Q: Or seek it?

Daniel: You will seek it, because that's all you know to do.

Q: But that seems a paradox.

The Important Question   17

Daniel: It is; anything that contradicts thought is paradoxical. So now you come to a point when you're no longer looking for freedom — you'll experience it. Because what you were looking for was the known. You can't look for something unknown; you will only impose a condition on life.

Q: *Until you experience that, would you be in conflict then? Because you're always batting yourself against the head, seeking something that can't be sought.*

Daniel: Traditionally we've tried to overcome the conflict; but now I understand that the conflict is the message. The conflict is the indicator that you're tearing yourself apart, you're violating some basic law. You are in one place, and you're trying to run off somewhere else. You've imposed a condition called somewhere else, or out there, and therefore you are living a life of pursuit and pressure. So you haven't come to the first recognition; the first recognition would be that you are the body. If you realize that, then you're no longer limited to the body; the body will free you, the body will release you.

You see, if I abandon my children or responsibilities to go off someplace, then I'll have my memories of the children when I arrive, and I'll see I haven't really left; something still calls me, I was not free to go. So there is a basic conflict. I haven't prepared for the journey; at the same time that I'm making a journey, I don't have the capacity to realize what I need. My body is not able to. I haven't introduced myself to my body. The passageway from mind or intellect to heart hasn't opened; the female and male aspects haven't merged. So I still move in division, I still move in opposites; and any time I move in opposites, there's going to be a tearing, a rupture someplace. That rupture I can call ill health, or conflict; it will take many shapes. Outwardly it may take the form of tragedy or collapse; inwardly it may take the form of tension or disease. I'll seek to have it cured, but the very cures I try are in fact increasing, or worsening the condition. Because obviously, all I can do actively is to put a bandage on it. What I can do is to better myself. But the bettering is the problem now. Bettering gives me the impression that this modification is change; but I'm still attached to the prior condition — I have not realized what is going on. Without that realization, I must live in conflict.

Now this conflict is the entire history. I am an extension of the entire history of humankind. And I have also been computerized, programmed to carry on that tradition. Even in reaction I carry on that tradition. Carrying on that tradition will always be conflict, will always be hurt. The hurt is the fact, the hurt is the signal that indicates that the movement is untrue, impure. And the forms that we've developed to discover freedom are actually perpetuating further bondage.

Questioner: I take a method on to ultimately free myself from that method, to be free. And what I'm getting from you is that that's an illusion, and I have to leave that alone.

Daniel: It's not that you have to leave it alone; understand what you're doing with that. If in fact you understand that you've only adopted techniques or approaches to be free from the technique or approach, then you can understand that you're a problem-maker — while you hope some day to solve all your problems. The real solution to the problem is not to start a new one. So you come to a point where you see that you're addicted to techniques, because your technique is your safety. But that safety is also your prison. You see, if you have an innocence in using the technique, that would be something; but you know from the beginning that the technique is a failure. That's clever — you have found a way to continue. You have found a way to use time to survive; you are continuing your domination through time. So in fact you're divorced from your body, you're divorced from the basic affection necessary for life. Because what you're doing with the technique is tormenting your body. You know in the first moment the failure of the technique, and yet you're inflicting it on your body.

This is always the fundamental challenge — how you've treated yourself, how you've treated the life form. If you haven't treated the life form in a balanced way, then there will always be a question of your integrity. If you try to kill yourself, what do you destroy but the form? So, great concern and affection for the form is a needed step, is a fundamental step for fulfillment in life. Because this form is also your instrument for further realization. It is not the sole thing, but it is primary. Because if the form is not living in health, not living without friction, you're not free to go, not free to experience.

So you may say that through the failure of your new technique, you will reach another plateau — but you've arrived, you see.

Q: *At first, let's say, I take a technique, and I realize that the technique isn't really my path, that it's just something I'm taking with me along the path.*

Daniel: But where are you going? You see, again, the path implies that there's a here and there. So the very here and there is time and space. My feeling would be that you're putting off the understanding through that approach, by creating a there that you will achieve some day; we use this path. I would say that you've arrived, you see. But we further the illusion by creating this time and space goal. 'The path' is in fact an attempt to get away from the realization.

If one can really observe what one is doing, the mind is seen to be a survival instrument — that's all it knows at this point, to survive. And we are programmed to survive, to carry on this sort of time-capsule, this guided missile; we have this collected information, and inherent in the genes, the genetic structure, is the urge to perpetuate it. So we try to find a way to perpetuate it, repeatedly. But the very perpetuation of that dominating center called 'me' is also the separation from the essence. One is dissipating their energies in that perpetuation.

So I see that I have invented a tomorrow, have invented a path, invented ways and roads and approaches — and I see that this very inventiveness is a running away. Understanding that is essential. Without that realization there's no life. Now if in fact you are innocent, and you didn't know the limitation of the approach, then I would say that the approach could be a necessary experience; you didn't know any better. But if in fact you've experienced the sorrow and pain already, then there is a lack of real affection if you again have to experience sorrow and pain. You're using sorrow and pain as a vehicle, but you're creating scars. Now many of us have come to feel or think that sorrow and pain is necessary. But when you are creating sorrow or pain because you think it's necessary, you are only torturing yourself. The realization of what you're doing is the introduction to clarity, to a flowering — but a flowering which is not taking place in time and space.

You see, it's very difficult to convey it unless we're moving together. The awareness of the need is a perception that happens in the moment. The manifestation that comes out of that perception is a flowering that appears to happen in time but it is not bound by time. What is bound by time is goal-orientation, projection, and pursuit. But now you're no longer pursuing any state; there is no state, there is nothing to achieve. But you may be introduced.

Essentially, a human being has no name, no definition, and there's no stopping point. But time and time and time again, you'll attempt to stop. When you attempt to stop, you'll again realize the lack. That lack again introduces you to the need to go deeper. Anything you achieve will still be limited. But you may desire to have feedback for yourself. So at times you may even find yourself describing your achievements; you'll say "I'm no longer eating meat", or "I'm able to run three miles now", or "I'm experiencing that"; there's an attempt to define it. There's an attempt to have a name for yourself — some definition, something to hang on to, some reference point. You have to be careful. It doesn't mean that you fight against it. The mind, as brain, is always seeking an orderly process, and it seeks it through a categorization. But what happens in that categorization is also a form of stagnation. So when the being sees the need, the name is no longer an imposition; the name is a dynamic that introduces.

There's a great need to understand in life. And a point comes where inherent in being alive is understanding. Understanding is taking place in simply being alive. If you realize that quality in your life, you will also realize that going deeper is simply to be alive — in everything you do, going deeper is inherent. You don't go deeper; deeper is a fact. You go deeper by breathing, you go deeper in your heartbeat, you go deeper as your blood circulates, you go deeper in eating, in sleeping. The very things that were boring to you at one point are now the dynamic, because you are now dynamic.

Questioner: *What happens when the forms are no longer separated from the formless? When form merges with formless, what kind of a perspective within life takes place? What's the outcome, or the product?*

Daniel: It's to be discovered. There's no outcome. Obviously form is an indication that something exists, that a quality exists. So form is not something to believe in; form is an introduction. Through the form we are introduced to something deeper. And if there's a keen intensity and awareness, then the introduction is unending. So there's no contradiction in terms any longer. Form indicates a quality of energy. That quality of energy is formlessness.

Q: *Why have you said that a human being is nothing?*

Daniel: Because we've gone through something to nothing. First you have a personal history — all the somethings that you define yourself by, and all the somethings that you also torment yourself by. And at one point you come to understand that this is merely the paraphernalia of the outer structure; then you're introduced to another quality. So all these somethings introduced you to nothing. And what I mean by nothing, is that there is no description — no definition, no category that fully describes a human being.

Q: *Not even energy?*

Daniel: Energy, only in terms of explanation; but not as self-description, you see — when you say, "Ah, yes, I'm energy."

22   in that stillness . . .

Q: *The formless energy?*

Daniel: The formless energy is again your construct, you see; it's another attempt to have a definition of self. But you may express it in that language to someone when you're talking. Language still can be a dynamic; it's not limited. When people say there's a limitation in the words, no — there's not; there's a limitation in the intensity, that's all.

Q: *In the receptivity.*

Daniel: The receptivity, and the intensity. But you can never blame the receptivity for the lack in communication. When your need is to communicate, then even though it may be relatively true that the receptivity is lacking, you must understand that your capacity to communicate is lacking.

Questioner: *Would you say that there's a limitation in the thinking of the words?*

Daniel: We've imposed a condition on the word. You see, at one point in life, sound was a pure energy of communication. Language is a development of that sound; the more sophisticated mind created a more sophisticated form called language. Language explained, it broke down, it structured; but still it was relatively simple because it still was a form of communication. But at one point in time, human beings became a threat to themselves. Then language became a form of deception, societal deception, not a form of communication any longer. What started as communication in the pure form, through expression in time, became deception.

   When you understand that whole structure of deception, at that point the language can also be restored as a tool of communication. It is not limited; we've limited it. It is only as limited as you are. It may be that you come to the end of language or the word and to the introduction of something else. It may be — whether that's a need or not, I don't know. It may be that the relationship develops to such an intensity that the word is not necessary. But I don't know that we should anticipate that day or even hope for it; if in fact that's the case, language will fall away of its own accord. But to me, inherent in the language is silence. And silence can be heard by someone who is moving at the same frequency.

16 August 1979

The Need for Essence

We spend most of our lives looking for something — we acquire and acquire and acquire, and whatever we acquire still does not seem to provide or fulfill; and still we search for something to fulfill us. And we turn our search to a God, to spirituality, to ethical philosophy, to helping the planet, to helping the race; and this also doesn't seem to provide the answer. It seems that nothing basically has changed, but that the outer circumstance is modifying its behavior, that's all; we're just putting on different costumes, or different ideas, or different faces, or whatever; and we're just proceeding along in the same way.

Now at times there may be a great collapse of everything you've constructed. And at times you may also wake up to one fact — that even the search for God and love is unclear. You're not godly inside, and you're not lovely; and that's precisely why you're searching for God and love. And precisely why we're searching for an accumulation is because we're empty. So there may be one moment in your life when everything collapses; and in that collapse, you can see a central fact — it is the emptiness, the ungodliness, the unloveliness that is searching; and in that search it has made everything a joke or an absurdity. It can use words like love and God very freely, but inside itself it may be quite insecure and frightened, and so therefore it has projected a God who takes care of all frightened people, who comes to the rescue.

So at a certain point one may be introduced to the ludicrousness of the whole construct. One may see that it's the same thing over and over and over again. One may be confronted with their whole life, and their whole dream, and their whole scheme and whole

The Need for Essence 25

idea system; and actually find out, in that moment, that what they have been doing all their life doesn't add up to much. But to me that is not a moment of despair. You may feel despair before you experience that, as a part of mind's pressure not to have you see it. But the actual experience of the mediocrity of our existence is the introduction to a quality — because you are no longer required to play that game once you recognize that it is a game. You're no longer required to invest all your energies in this performance, this circular performance. At the moment that you see what has been, and what will be, coming from the past, you have the opportunity to step out of time — by simply realizing the need.

At that moment I see that the need is to touch something real. I see that the need is to have something of quality, to live in quality; and yet I don't know what reality is, and I don't know what quality is, because until that moment all I had were ideas of reality. I've never experienced a reality, I've only experienced my ideas of what I think reality is, what I think love is, what I think the world is, what I think God is — they're my ideas that I've played with, that I've pondered. Reality cannot be pondered, love cannot be pondered, God cannot be pondered; only the ideas that we have can be pondered. When I have actually seen the futility of my ideas, I yearn for something real. At that moment I step out of the structure of idea. I'm still alive, I'm still breathing, I'm still a functioning, dynamic human being; but I am no longer bound in time and space, I'm no longer bound in history — because I've recognized a need. I need to live fully — simply put. When I recognize the need to live fully, I touch an energy that has always existed, that has always been available — but that I have simply never recognized. That recognition can only take place in stillness; because that energy is stillness, and the recognition of that energy can only happen in stillness. So, at that moment, what I am recognizing is what I am. I am touching a quality in myself.

Now some of us may experience that we touch that, for a moment, and yet it seems to disappear. We felt what seemed to be fullness, dependent on nothing — not a thought, not an idea, not depending on anyone's smile or good will, or any of that. And then some event takes place; something happens, and you don't feel it. For some, the absence of that quality, once experienced, leads them into despair, or an attempt to define their lives around the memory of that experience.

So the experience indicates the possibility; but if the experience is no longer taking place as a dynamic, then that experience has actually confined me, defined me, limited me. I experience something here this evening, and then I go to my room and it's gone. Mechanically what I'll do is try to come back here and have that experience again. So when I go to my room and experience the lack, I also experience in that moment a greater need — and that is to experience that in my room also.

Now some of you, in the last month or so, have experienced a quality of stillness, in the moment, and then a short time later you'll experience what appears to be old familiar mechanical behavior. When I experience that behavior, I experience a great need to find something that's trustworthy, or find something that's real. The absence of that reality is more than I can bear; I can't bear it now. So what is the obvious need?

When I move through life, I see the need is to experience that essence. And as I touch that essence more and more, each time I don't feel it I feel a greater need, a greater yearning. And each time I feel this greater yearning, I also experience the need to touch that quality again. And a great refinement is taking place in that, physically and psychologically; and also a great refinement is happening around one. Now I experience an energy that transforms. The very yearning is a journey, and the very journey transforms. By transforming I mean that something new is happening physically, something new is happening in the brain. When you see something new, there's also something new in you. When you are able to see something brand new, without a name — clearly — there is also a new quality in your own brain. A mutation has taken place. Something that was sleeping or dormant is now alive in one. Having seen it, you look for it — you look for it now. In the past you saw faces, in the past you saw a posture, in the past you just walked through the crowd; now you're seeing some quality in life, it's a bit more than just faces. There's no philosophy around it, it's just a bit more. But having seen it now, you're introduced to a greater urgency, a greater need to see more. As you're seeing it, it's changing for you, and you're changing to meet that change. And every time you're denied that sight in any way — any time that you have a hint that there's something more — each time you yearn again. You again formulate your need. To me, realizing the need is the only relationship; it's the only healing, the only understanding.

So that yearning takes you on a journey. And in that journey you pass through all the milestones of life. At one point you come to realize where you're going. And as you come to realize where you're going, the capacity to wait is great, because you're introduced at that moment to what must be. You know, in sitting in one place, that you're moving toward the source. You know, in just sitting still, that you're moving to the essence always. At that moment you see the whole question of relationship and family; you see the whole question of relationship to food, to illness; you see the answer to the whole social and human question. In fully recognizing this need to live — that we can't live in this past-future structure, this prison of repetition any longer — then the relationships that you've established will also facilitate that realization. If you recognize your need for freedom, your need for love, your need to touch a quality of reality, then in recognizing your need you'll also allow those with you to experience that. In not recognizing your need, you'll replace that quality with yourself in relationship to the other. We replace this energy of God with ourselves. If you recognize your need to be free, you'll also experience a family that will be free — not through anything you do, but simply through recognizing your need. If you recognize that need, then the family introduces you to a greater sensitivity and a greater essence in your life. So obviously everything has freedom in it, and everything has bondage in it — depending on what you need. If you desire security from your creation, then you will create bondage for yourself. But if you yearn for freedom and essence, then the very family structure you've created will also introduce you to that quality.

We've come to a point in our enquiry where we can recognize that the understanding is itself the change. The realization of the need in fact puts everything into motion. And now one comes to a point where one needs to live in this essence, this quality always. And when you put the question that way, it's always granted — always. And you come to realize that it has not occurred before because you've never asked for it, you've never realized the need. Each step along the way, you come to realize the greater need, and as you realize the greater need, a transformation is taking place, in every moment. That to me is the relationship, the only relationship. Having heard it, having experienced it in our life, we lead a choiceless existence. Relationship is our mutual need to touch on a quality that is real, that is consistent — that is eternal.

2 September 1979

A Life in Freedom

Questioner: I see that I've been searching in my life, but I'm not sure for what.

Daniel: When the search is over, that's when I feel life begins. When I say the search is over, I mean that you realize in your life that searching actually dissipates the energy. But when you need, without searching being available to you, then all the energy that went out into the seeking is now conserved. Then you're waiting in that intensity. When you are searching, what are you looking for?

Q: Peace.

Daniel: Where can you get it? Who has it? When you realize that what you're looking for is not man-made; when you realize that it cannot be gotten by the same old way that we do business, cannot be gotten through effort, through pressure, out of fear; when you realize that you're looking for something which if it's not man-made must be divine, must have some quality — if no one has it, and the need is great, then you're left with understanding your need, and asking for it.

Q: If I understand my need, I think there's nothing to ask.

Daniel: Because understanding the need, and asking, are one movement.

Q: Right.

Daniel: The whole body, everything; when the heart and the mind and the whole being understand the need, it's a total movement. The very yearning, the very understanding of the need is the response. What you've been looking for cannot be gotten through the way you know to move, to operate; you can only find the known with the known. And yet you're looking for something that's unknown. Peace is an eternal quality — something that cannot be pursued.

So to understand the need is to focus. And when it's focused, the whole being is present. In your planning for a family, in whatever you're doing — focus, see the need, understand it. You have an effect in your life, and the lives around you, and you also have the capacity to touch on a new quality. So there must be a refinement, there must be a sharpness, there must be an alertness. If clarity is to come out of it, if love is to come out of it, then life must be approached with that intensity.

With that intensity, one is no longer bound in history, no longer shackled to history, no longer bound to repeat the past. A human being is a being who in every movement is free, and expresses that freedom. And that freedom can only be touched when you recognize the need for it. When you recognize the need for it in your own life, you'll also come to recognize that there's a need for it in every life. Life needs to be free if we're to be fully alive. Each movement that freedom makes is also free.

So if we've shared anything, it's that each person can be introduced to the potential they have in their life. But the recognition of the need to realize that potential is up to each individual. Can one simply live in this quality of stillness, where one can know deeply that it's all right, that life is not a threat — not positive thinking, or negative thinking, or any of these things; just clearly understand that it's all right — that death, life, sickness, all these things, are not threats.

Can the simple person be holy? Once I realize it's possible to live that free existence, how can I live with any less? Once you recognize the need, it must come. Life is not life without that freedom now. As long as I thought that what I was doing was life, then I lived within that structure; but now I realize it's not life at all — that I've yet to live. To realize that it's all sleepwalking, it's all daydreaming, is to yearn to wake up.

Questioner: Basically, it seems that what ages is mind, through memory and projection. When we're born again — not in a Christian sense, but in this sense of coming alive — is there still aging in life?

Daniel: Maybe; it's still subtle. You see, the child is given birth only in thought, the child is thought. The person, this form, everything in this room is a product of thought; the whole history of humankind, history is thought itself. So anything that is conceived in thought is also thought, is also bound by thought. So, what we take to be childhood, what we take to be adulthood, in fact is the thought. These things haven't happened, have not actually happened — they've only happened within the construct of thought.

Q: So the body responds as thought moves.

Daniel: So the body is thought-bound, and that thought knows a birth and a death. It knows illness, it knows collapse, it knows everything that thought knows. That's what the body is, and that's what the world around us is. So when I realize that I am thought, and I cannot be more than thought, and everything I do will be bound in that history, I realize in that moment that I have not lived at all. You see, the potential is there for divinity, the potential is there for newness, but we come to think of this potential as the fact. It's not the fact; we are living only within the thought structure. We are personally, physically, the creation of thought.

Q: In time.

Daniel: And bound in time. And when I see that limitation, I do yearn for something beyond that, not bound in that. That yearning is the introduction to something not bound in thought. So now, does that quality — not bound in thought — know aging? Does it know death? Let's see — because the possibility, then, is that aging is a memory, and death is a memory. So do we still need to die and age? I don't know — let's see how deep it goes. We know that what we call death and aging and sickness has happened, that no one as far as we can see in our history has escaped it. So I'm not interested in escaping it, but I'm also questioning now whether it's necessary to age, whether it's necessary to die, whether it's necessary to live within that structure any longer — the structure of thought moving through time and space.

Questioner: I have read, and people I have spoken with have said they believe, that there really have been some people who have gone beyond that — that there were some people who had lived for perhaps thousands of years.

Daniel: But thousands of years is still limited.

Q: But this would still be a present condition — these people haven't died.

Daniel: I don't know; you see, people may have said it, you may have heard it; but I haven't seen it. I've heard of possibilities, and they may or may not be true. But now in our own lives we may be introduced to a possibility. I see that the logical extension of what is being said is the absence of illness, aging, and death. The premise would be that if death is a memory, and sickness and aging are memory, then this memory, perceived, can also be wiped away or cleared.

Q: We're talking of a new form now.

Daniel: So, we are; we're talking about a mutation, but it hasn't happened. Let's see how thorough the understanding is. Once you awaken to the need, you put something in motion. But let's see how thorough that awakening is. You may realize the need, but you may not have the physical surroundings that will allow for it.

A *Life in Freedom* 33

My premise is that if you realize the need, it will have to come to pass; it must. So if you realize the need not to have illness in your life, you still may be subject to illness, but it doesn't mean change is not occurring.

The historical pressure is great. Everything we've done and will do — our entire background — is history, and we're bound by it. The entire life is programmed. All the information is contained in the brain and in the cells, and we're bound by that information.

Is there a life beyond that information? Do you need a life beyond that information? Only when you come to understand the limitation of living life in a programmed way is there a need in you to be fresh and vital. How thorough, how intense is the need, and the realization of that need, let's see.

So I may see that there's a need for no physical death. But the question is, do we actually see these needs in our lives? It's very important that what is being said does not become undigested information. You see, if the need was just food, it would be so much clearer to us. If you are really hungry and you see the need for food, it's so clear. But the need for immortality is not so clear; you're not directly confronted with crisis that often. It's only when you're confronted with great illness or the possibility of death that you may see a need for immortality. So we only know to move from fear, we never move from clarity; it's only when we're threatened with the loss of something that we start to see the need. But now can this movement take place out of intelligence?

Questioner: We see the need for immortality, and to be healthy and alive — but the body has been conditioned for millions of years to live, to die, go through that cycle. From the time I really perceive this need, how long does it take to manifest?

Daniel: I see that I'm historically bound, I see I'm a product of the past, and I see that I'm conditioned over millions of years to continue the same thing — I see it. And when I see it, there's no old age. Old age is not the aging of the body, not the movement of the body; old age is the psychological fear that accompanies it. So old age is fear; young age is fear. Aging is fear — that's all. But my concern is freedom; my concern is that whatever age I am, I'm alive, I'm free. That happens in the moment. Now the physical effect of that realization may be seen in time.

Q: *You may not see it, though.*

Daniel: It may not be; I don't know. That is not my personal concern. But one can see immortality; immortality is to live in the minute, so thoroughly, that this minute is my universe. That to me is immortality — each second is a lifetime. And if each second is a lifetime, a lifetime is millions of years — I'm immortal in that. But now physically, will there be an expression that corresponds with that understanding? Let's see. The premise is yes, there must be. But physically, let's see if it's so. The premise is that a free human being is no longer subject to memory — the memory of illness, the memory of aging, even the memory of death.

Let's see if it's actually so. Once we've discovered that possibility, it may come about. If it doesn't come about with me personally, then it may come about with others. I may realize it personally, but it's not my personal need. It's humankind's need. At one point in your life you start to understand that your personal need is also a universal need; that where the individual perceives, the collective can also realize. So you can say that the individual at that point is actually abandoning himself — is actually free to go, free to travel, free to explore anything. Life is unfettered.

9 September 1979

A Love That is True

Many people ask me, what's your purpose, what's being communicated, what am I doing in relationship to others and what does it all mean? I find that in my life, certain incidents occurred that forced me to awaken to the need to experience, or to realize something that was full and true. I came to realize a need in my personal existence to reach my potential, to understand what this life is first-hand. And until that moment, I realize, it had not been life at all; it was just a series of movements that I took to be life. It was only in awakening to that need that I experienced something I can call actually living. And I saw in that quality of living, that it was not only my personal need, but that it was in fact a human need — a need in all human beings to awaken to that quality. At one time in my life I awakened to a need for real love — something real, a quality of love and affection that can be felt. And I may only awaken to that need through sorrow, through the failure of all previous attempts. And when I awaken to that need for a love that is true, a love that is full, I can stand the test of time with that quality. The absence of that quality in my life, I recognize to be the cause of great stress and hurt; and by extension I recognize that the cause of stress and hurt in society or collectively is also that absence.

So when I experience my need to awaken to a love that is full and true, I also experience a connection to all of life, to all of humanity. And in experiencing my need to awaken to that quality, I also experience the need for humanity to awaken to that quality. Only when there is a mutual recognition of that need could you say that there is community. To me, then, community is the realization of the need, the realization or the understanding of that need to experience fullness, touch fullness; to immerse oneself in a full love, a full life.

When that realization is full, this then becomes life's meaning, life's purpose. It's not that one takes on a mission, not that someone takes up a standard to identify themselves with. It's that one realizes that in fact they are that purpose. When you awaken to the need, every action that seemed to be a simple action in the past, is now infused with that understanding, charged with that need. So every action that one takes is a further flowering, a further unfolding, a further introduction. Until that awakening is full, we haven't lived at all.

In this unfolding, in this flowering, there is nothing final — life is a constant unfolding; it has a quality of constant introduction. But until one awakens the need to experience something of quality, to experience a life of freedom, to realize a potential, the journey can't really begin. Now this journey is not one which is bound in time and space, that has a fixed goal in the future. The journey that I'm speaking of is a journey of increased capacity to recognize *what is*. It is not a journey that covers distance, that is bound by time. It is a journey of sensitivity. As one realizes, one is also introduced to a further realization.

So as one proceeds, one is also developing, one is also sensitizing, one is also refining. What you see outwardly now transforms you inwardly. What you're seeing outwardly is changing; it appears to have changed because you're seeing qualities in it that before you have never seen. And as you are able to see these qualities, it indicates that there is a sensitivity growing in you that is allowing that perception to take place. So this is then what I mean by a journey not bound by time and space, not moving according to time. What we have called birth and life can actually be the preparation before the journey. In retrospect, I see that in fact everything that I've done in this so-called life has actually been a certain sort of preparation; the excess, the residue, the baggage is being put aside. So the actual journey takes place when one is no longer an obstacle to one's life, when one is no longer creating a barrier to understanding. The journey takes place only when one is free to go, when one is no longer psychologically bound.

A Love That is True

Now each movement, each action that takes place in life is allowing one to see, to go a bit deeper: the simplest incident — the play of light, the raindrop, the child's face, the tears, the fears. As you proceed, life intensifies. Something is actually changing inside of you; there's a quality of change that is happening which allows the perception. The perception cannot take place until that quality of change is there.

Questioner: Can you be more specific as to what it is that intensifies?

Daniel: As I awaken to a need through the sorrow and the limitation of everything I've experienced — awaken to a need for something vital, for something true — there's a great curiosity in me to look, to see. And I also understand the limitation of trying to seek out something real. When I awaken to that need, I no longer have the capacity to seek. I experience a quality of life that heretofore was unknown to me. It comes at the end of seeking.

So with that intensity I look. Now I perceive what appears to be light — a quality of light. When I look I see light. When I see that light so strongly, there is a tremendous attraction; there is a tremendous further yearning, there is an intense yearning to immerse oneself in that light. That movement — which again, is not a movement through time and space — is a movement of understanding, of perception. As you see the light, there is a quality emerging in you that is equal to the quality of what you perceive. The quality in you yearns to merge with that. When you experience that urgency to merge, there is no other life. When you experience that urgency to merge, you awaken to your true purpose, to your true meaning. And as you understand your meaning, you also understand the purpose of life itself. When you awaken to the need to merge, you also awaken to the need in all humanity to merge.

23 September 1979

The Face of Love

We'll never be happy, we'll never be full until we realize the extent of God's love. Until you realize thoroughly that you are loved, there's always going to be discontent — difficulties, this feeling of something lacking, insecurity and fear and the desire to have something. And yet the quality of God's love is not something that is a demonstrative love, it's not something loud or stimulating. God's love has always relied on its obviousness, on its apparentness, and the ability of an individual to see what is obvious, to see what is apparent. It seems to take time. One apparently has to go through the whole structure, the whole limitation of psyche. One in fact must go through the whole history of humankind before they can realize that there's a love that waits, that there's a quality of love that's reliable, that can be counted on; there is no longer a need for any expectation, because any expectation that one has will not be enough. So the whole expectation syndrome becomes absurd also in the face of love. In that expectation we've turned it into some sort of object or toy, and we lose the capacity to touch the vastness involved.

And yet I see that insecurity, that fear, that desire, that expectation, that desire for feedback must carry on, it must — until one is able to realize the fullness of this universal love; until one is touched with that quality so thoroughly that there is no longer fear. One is not dependent on feedback or expectation of support, because they realize essentially that what they are, the whole fact of being alive is love — and they are one with that. When the heart awakens, when the being awakens to the need, there is the understanding that one is immersed in this quality that one has been seeking all one's life. What one has been looking for is right here — it exists. But before that recognition, you're going to suffer from the social problems. I see the need to be free, the need to be unbound, without limitation. And so therefore I find it very important in my life that all my relationships, everything I've created, is in great order, is sane, is clear. And any time I move, I move with understanding, I move with intensity; in all my relationships, as far as I'm concerned, it's clear how we're related and what the need is. I need to live a life that's unbound, that's unlimited, I need to touch a quality of vastness. And each action I take must facilitate that exploration, that journey. So each time I relate to someone I call my child, or my mother or father, or my friend or my lover, I must make sure that I'm moving in an orderly way. And then when we depart, we depart in order, with intelligence. If I'm to discover the essence of life, that's my concern.

When the life I'm living is precious to me, then all of life is precious to me; I'm not going to entangle myself psychologically, I'm not going to fix myself to one circumstance, paralyze myself. My need is to live, and I recognize that all life needs to express that quality. So, in each act, with anyone, can I see the need, simply see the need — that's all we are talking about.

So I see in my life that it is not possible to depend on anyone for feedback and support; it is not possible any longer that I depend on my society, my race, my color, my religion, or any organization for my well-being. I need to touch the source, the essence of well-being. And only in touching that essence can I say that I have an intelligent relationship with all humanity, with all of life. Without touching that essence, everything that I've created is in question. I see that there is a need for that light to exist in all relationship, in everything that I'm involved in. And so when I am talking to anyone, when I'm involved with anyone, I look for that light. If I'm going anywhere — to visit a relative, or to visit a friend, or to do something, I'm clear what I'm doing. And if I'm now proceeding in a marriage, I'm clear what the quality of that marriage is. And if I set out in this agreement with another, and we feel a love so strong that we feel a need to bring a child into this life, it will have to be clear. There's a great need in me not to create any more scars on this earth, any more pain on this earth, any more difficulties on this earth; so it is something that I'll weigh, examine, feel. And only then, when it is clear and full, will I participate in it fully.

When I see the need in my life to live purely and fully, I am also taking action that will facilitate that purity, that fullness. That is the actual communication or sharing in life. That comes when one touches upon the actual meaning or purpose of life, and is living it in every action. That is when one is merged with divinity, and each action is divine.

So there's a need for divinity, there's a need for vastness, and I recognize that need. In that fullness there's no separation, there's no expectation, there's no desire. When the relationship is full, there's no actual separation. So when one is moving in full cooperation, everything that one does is coming out of a love they're feeling. They don't need expectation, they don't need praise. Praise may come, it may not come; but that is no longer the basis of the relationship. Feedback is no longer the measurement, the basis for the relationship, for why I do things. Having experienced this vastness, I am no longer looking to extract or to extort substance from another. When I love, I love unconditionally.

When I see the need to be free, I also see the need for freedom in the life around me. When I see the need for vastness, and a life without limitations, without these neurotic imposed conditions, I am no longer imposing that condition on my children. So when I see the need for freedom, I also see the human need for freedom. When I see my need to touch upon an essence in life, I also see the need, in relationship to my children, to have that essential quality express itself. Now marriage and children are my introduction to vastness.

So I see the need; I see the need to live in fullness in my life, and therefore I see the need to introduce that fullness in every action. It's a need now, not a goal or an idea; it's an actual need in life. Then the entire life is a dynamic quality. Every action therefore is a sadhana, every action is a meditation. And every relationship that is established with that intensity is a relationship that facilitates that looking, that learning, that understanding.

Questioner: Is it possible that one person in a relationship can be acting from need, and another not?

Daniel: One person acting in clarity, moving from clarity, will introduce clarity into the household. It's a question of time.

Q: So either it will come clear, or it will not continue?

Daniel: It won't continue.

Q: So then the person who is insane will become sane?

Daniel: What we've called insanity was a position that one took within a given circumstance. When that circumstance is no longer there, then there's no longer a requirement to be what is called insane or imbalanced. Insanity is merely an attempt to survive in a hostile world. If one clearly sees that there's no longer a need for it, then the behavior is out of context.

When the child is demonstrating a certain kind of behavior that appears to be anti-social or destructive, then the child is indicating to us that we haven't provided a full quality. We have not been able to demonstrate that there's no need for extortion or pressure.

If in the midst of this relationship you wake up to a greater need — that there's a need for freedom in your life, and therefore there's a need for freedom in this relationship — then you're no longer bound by the role, you're no longer historically bound. You've introduced intelligence into your life, into the relationship. And you're no longer susceptible to the pressures that come out of the psyche. There's no fear of loss; there's nothing to gain. Then you can relate, then you can find a means of communication. Communication takes place in freedom. Communication happens from heart to heart — when the heart is open. When one recognizes their life in the other, when one recognizes themselves in the other, there is no other.

So when you are speaking to your child, you're actually speaking to your heart. Anytime you feel your heart open, anytime you feel that softness in your life, that softness, that quality of stillness indicates that you're also speaking to all relationships. When you feel your heart, you're also related to all of humanity, to all of life. That is the quality I'm speaking of. So the action you take is an action coming out of that quality of heartfulness; you feel your heart. You're no longer depending on the feedback from the activity — because everything that you can receive in life, you already are receiving. When the heart is opened, the action that comes out of that is an expression of love. When the heart is open in such a way, the relationships that you've established will also touch a new dimension in life, a new quality. And as you move now into different facets of the social existence, you're introduced to new qualities. You'll approach it all with this fullness of heart, and then everything you're doing is sharing that; it's not even a question of your wanting to share that. As far as you're concerned you're moving from this feeling, and everything you do is an expression of that feeling.

Now you may run into a circumstance, either in the family, or socially, or in business, that is a limit, that introduces you to your limitation. Then what you felt as full-heartedness is limited; it's not enough. The actual outer condition has not responded. Now you are confronted with a further challenge in your life. What you experienced in the prior moment to be fullness, you now experience to be a limitation.

Questioner: That fullness is being tested.

Daniel: So let's understand what's taking place. Fullness now is a limitation. And that limitation introduces you to the need for a greater expansion. So that obstacle, or so-called obstacle, is actually the opportunity to let the love deepen. The resistance that we meet in the society around us introduces us to a need for a greater love. Then I understand how intricate it all is, how blended it all is, how balanced it all is. The so-called resistance, I now understand, introduces me to a need to experience a depth.

Having this human structure of thought, we can't believe that we're loved; we know we're not loveable. We give God these attributes of thought; we've created a god like ourselves, and since we have preference, we also have invented a God that has preference. But when you touch on an energy or an essence that is without attributes, without preference, then you feel a great need. In the face of that love, there's a great need in you to be lovely.

12 October 1979

Passages

The following passages have been drawn from larger public talks.

Ego is the known. When you understand the false, you have come to the end of the known, you have touched stillness. Now take a deep look. You can see a different quality now. When you come to the end of the known you touch upon stillness. Through that stillness you will understand compassion, passion, yearning, essence, love — and still it goes on. But the first step is to see the false.

* * *

17 June 1979

By going through the intellect, and beyond, we're being introduced to a new innocence — not the innocence of not knowing, but the innocence of understanding — that knowledge divorced from essence is not enough.

* * *

2 July 1979

Throughout history, humankind has attempted to touch something meaningful, to find some purpose in life. Throughout recorded history we see a desire to understand, a desire to love, a desire to merge, a desire for completion of one sort or another; a constant looking for meaning and purpose. The religious teachings of most societies seem to express that yearning, to focus on it. In Judaism, there's a great yearning for the messenger of God — the son of God, the Messiah, the savior — to lift humankind above its petty or mediocre limitations. In Hindu scriptures it was sometimes expressed as the female, Shakti, yearning for Shiva, the lord of the universe. And in simple terms, with someone like Kabir, the mystic poet, the yearning for God was expressed through himself as the bride, and the lord, God, as the bridegroom; and life had no meaning until that merger took place. So it seems that the religious history indicates or posits that yearning is essential. It also gives one a glimpse into the possibilities that there is something beyond the mundane, that there is some quality which is divine. And for the few individuals who have approached this, there was no other life but God — without the response of the beloved, they had no life, life had no meaning. When one came to understand that there was a lack, that one was living a life without essence, a life without love, one couldn't go on any longer in the same way. It was an empty shell. Whatever one might accomplish had no meaning.

Now in this modern age, we've also attempted to supply meaning — through achievement, through goals, through acquisition, through position. That may have lasted for a period of time, but it seemed essentially that the same thing was lacking. Mind, divorced from essence, projects; and it only projects material, matter — something to run after in the future, something to be accomplished in the future. In fact, the religions that have now developed are also religions of projection — that through good works one will attain a certain state, or attain God; or that after death one will achieve something beyond.

I come to a point personally in life when I see that in attempting to run after everything that I've been taught is meaningful — through acquisition, through belief systems, through support structures — something is still lacking. It doesn't mean that I haven't accomplished, it doesn't mean that I haven't achieved; I have achieved, physically and socially, whatever I've gone after. But in the achievement, I still come up with emptiness. What I learn from this emptiness is that the achievement, the accumulation of the outer, cannot supply me with what I need. When through failure, through sorrow or through pain I can no longer pursue the outer — because I realize its limitation — at that moment an inward journey takes place. When I cannot rely on the outer to provide me with substance, then I look at this entity called the self. I look at myself. And is my body of knowledge and information able to provide me with substance? Is there anything meaningful, is there anything I can depend on in my information? When I examine this entity I call myself thoroughly, I also see that it is fragmented; it also moves according to personal pleasure, it moves away from pain, it moves according to preference; it does whatever it's been taught to do. And I can't rely on it — I can't rely on its urges, its demands, its inclinations. So I see that the outer accumulation is still lacking, it doesn't fulfill; I can't rely on that accumulation for actual security. And when I look at this self-construct — 'me' — I also see that it can't provide anything of substance; it's limited. Essentially it doesn't know what is real, it doesn't know essence or substance.

So now, at this point, the outer accumulation and the inner information don't provide; they're useless. Then I come to an understanding that there's nothing to depend on, there's nothing to rely on that I know. In short, I come to the ending of 'me', the ending of the known. At that point, I come to understand what I've been doing for much of my life — I understand why this pursuit exists, why this accumulation of information exists, what I've been looking for. In this accumulation of information, I am trying to reinforce or support an entity in order to maintain something real and substantial, and I've discovered that I cannot acquire the real through the pursuit. The need is there, the yearning is there, but the expression is no longer available — because I see its limitation. So when I have actually come to this point and I am no longer wasting energy in unnecessary thought, in unnecessary accumulation of knowledge or things, I recognize what I am — because I yearn to, the yearning is there, the need is great. When I come to this moment, I am no longer an entity; I am pure yearning.

What is this yearning? To me, yearning only takes place when you understand that there's a lack — when the lack is so great, and so apparent — and there is no way, no known way to satisfy it. Then, when there's no known way to satisfy it — no escape from that situation, no getting out of it — one *is* yearning. In that yearning, one can feel, one can absorb the response. Only yearning has the receptivity to hear, to feel thoroughly.

It has been posited in the past that the female Shakti, once aroused, once feeling the need for love, yearns for her lover Shiva. And it is only when the yearning is so great that the counterpart called Shiva or God awakens as a response. Before this point God is a projection of thought, of conditioning. But when conditioning is no longer at play, when projection is no longer available — when a human being is fully yearning — this human being receives a response equal to what he is. In short, when the yearning is strong, one is both male and female. What I look for is what I am. But until that point is reached in my life, I cannot recognize God, I cannot recognize love — because I'm seeing it through the screen of the entity, the 'I', the conditioning. Without that response, life has no meaning, there is no security; in fact there is no God and there is no love. It is only when through yearning I have reached my full potential — when, in short, I am a human being — that God can respond. God is a response to a human being; the beloved is a response to the lover. If it is not taking place in one's individual existence, it is because the need is not formulated and recognized.

2 *July 1979*

* * *

Questioner: What is the state called "blissed out"?

Daniel: It's a concentration on form. Concentration is like a spotlight. When you shine a spotlight on any one thing, it illuminates that one thing, but everything else is in darkness. So it's a limited affair. Through that steady concentration, you can go into a trance state, or have a fixed form; you can call that blissed out. But what I mean by blissed out seems to be a necessary first step; and that is to be happy, to feel vital. I think it's dangerous to get fixed up in the point of happiness, where you personalize happiness to such an extent that at one point you build a wall around it. Then it ceases to be happiness; then it's fear. So I feel that happiness is an essential step to discovery, to understanding, to merger, or to love. But it is not the place itself. In fact, I don't see that there is a 'the' place. Life is unfolding, and each thing seen and understood is an introduction to a deeper understanding.

Since we have this habit of thinking that we have plenty of time, that there is a tomorrow, we never demand excellence; we don't have a taste for the essence of things. We have more of a taste for costumes and drama. Only when we are threatened with loss are we pressured to look for the essence. This is in line with the yogic texts which describe a phenomenom called *kundalini*, which posits that there is a female aspect called Shakti that sits at the base of the spine — a sleeping snake coiled three-and-a-half times. It is also posited that Lord Shiva, the lord of the universe, is sitting at the top of the head, and he is sleeping. His eyes are closed and he is just sitting in meditation. When Shakti is aroused, what arouses her is the understanding that love is not present. The arousal, or the need for love, only takes place when one understands that what one has been going through is not love at all — some essential quality is missing, and you know it; and you can't fill it in with all your activities, and you know that also.

So Shakti, the female energy, is dormant; and when she comes to understand that love is not there in her life — she sees it clearly — that absence creates a deep yearning. The yearning of Shakti creates the response called Shiva. Until Shakti yearns, there is no God, there is no male. The yearning female awakens the male. It's also said in many stories of Shiva and Shakti, that when Shakti is aroused, she needs Shiva; she can take no substitute. And there are many attempts by demons to trick her by taking on the form of Shiva. They even have sexual intercourse with her, but at the moment of climax she knows that it's not Shiva, she knows it's a demon. So she is able to tell, in her need, in her yearning, what is a correct response; she waits for the real essence — called Shiva. So when the yearning is great it turns into a passion, and the passion creates a response. Shiva would be the essence; essence is the response to the passion. When it is posited that a human being yearns for God, then God also yearns for a human being. But there is no God until one is a human being. There is no love until one yearns, until one needs love. But what we call love, what we call God, what we call relationship, what we call art, is not coming out of passion, or silence, or yearning; it's a form of stimulation. Stimulation will always have comparisons. But love will never be comparative. One may have a therapeutic existence, but love is not therapy; love is not something that helps people, not something that can be possessed by anyone. God has no qualities; it can't be used by anyone; it has no value. The mind can't own it, can't spend it, can't show it off. But without it there is no life.

* * *

13 July 1979

Anything that is not real cannot stand direct perception, direct looking. When there is a real interest in seeing, there is a total movement. When you bring that keenness and that intensity into any area, the area itself becomes enlightened. Only something that is real, that has substance, can withstand that light. The false is dissolved.

* * *

15 July 1979

Healing doesn't take place until you touch that quality of softness. What you can do is apply a temporary bandage. What you can do is to have an effect through suggestion. What you can do in a moment of crisis is to assert one ego over another temporarily until they can get over the pain. But the real healing force is only operating when a person has that passion; and the healing is a response to that passion. Without the passion, there's no cure, there's just medication. You see, the pain and the illness and the mental disturbance — they're a creation of the individual. The individual creates the mental disturbance, creates the illness, and will not let go of the illness so easily. The illness becomes very important to an ego that's afraid of being alone, afraid of boredom, afraid of seeing itself. But if you come to a point in your life where it's in fact not treatment that you need, but understanding, then that illness will teach you what you are. Then listen to it.

* * *
16 July 1979

You can only do what you're free to do in life. Without essential freedom, you can't really move very far. If you've left something undone, it has a call on you. The very memory of it calls you back. In the same way, meditation means that you're free to look — you are free to examine; you have no prior call. Meditation is not a therapeutic tool that you use to try to shut out the rest of the world. Meditation takes place when the condition is in order around you. All your obligations are fulfilled, as far as you can see, physically and socially; you are free to sit, you are free to enquire. And then secondly, the concern would be that there is no physical pain. The first meditation would be to see if anything calls you physically, if there is any disturbance.

When that condition is met — where the outer circumstance is in order as far as you can see, and physically there is no problem, there is no discomfort — only then can you enquire after the thought process. See what is happening psychologically, what you are thinking. And if there is no longer a disturbance physically or psychologically, then you may even enquire deeper physically, internally. And in this regard, when there is no disturbance physically at all, internally or externally, then you may also look into the so-called unconscious aspects of your thought — your pressures, your fears, your hopes, your dreams. It's just being viewed.

Freedom is essential to the meditation. That is what I mean by discovery being the basis for the meditation — discovery of freedom. Everything must be in order. And anything that calls you is the subject of your meditation. If it's a physical pain, respond to that. If it's a thought, respond to that — until you come to a point where there is no personal call. And then the sounds in the street and the sounds in your body become one. Respond to anything that calls you; be aware of it, listen to it, feel it. And when even the outward sounds no longer call you and there is no longer a sound inwardly that calls you, just be aware of the stillness. So meditation is simply that journey. And you'll find that every sound, every thought, every pressure, every sight, every breath, every heartbeat will take you deeper and deeper into it. It's all introduction at that point. Life is continually blossoming, unfolding, revealing deeper and deeper qualities of itself.

23 July 1979

* * *

I come to understand that I cannot hear, I cannot see, I don't allow myself to understand; that all I am experiencing is myself. It's an important point — that there is a separation between myself and what I see, there's always a description. I come to understand that all I'm doing every day is repeating my information, over and over and over again. I need to see and I cannot. I need to hear and I cannot. I'm mechanical. If I hear or see anything, the first thing that happens is that I categorize it, I know it. And I come to understand that I'm separate from all of life; I can't understand the depth of it.

At that point, I come to rest. I realize that what I see is what I am. All the definitions that I have are coming from me. I'm not seeing anything, I'm just seeing my own thought process. The outward stuff is just association for me. Every time I see something, it triggers something in my brain, and all I see is that picture inside, I don't see anything at all. I come to realize that I've never lived, I've never seen, I've never heard anything. The whole world is just existing in my brain.

At the point you start to be aware of that, the very awareness of that introduces you to a stillness. And when you are in this stillness and you look, what you're seeing you have never seen before. You are seeing that stillness also. Now ironically, still what you see is what you are — but you have undergone a change, and when you look with that change, the world around you has also undergone a change. Now the world around you is teaching you more about yourself. The change that has happened to you in that stillness is also happening around you. Everything you are doing from that point on is a dynamic, it takes you deeper — everything that is happening. There is no longer an inner and an outer movement. As far as language goes, as far as our understanding goes, it's inner and outer. But in fact there is no inner and outer. What you see is what you are; what is happening around you is happening inside you. The sound you hear has a corresponding effect inside of you. It's all moving together.

When you live in that, your action is true. There's no individual there, there is no personality there that is affected by it. Each action is clear and pure, without residue. At that point, you can say that there is no separation between the observer and the observed; there is no separation in any way. When there is no separation between what you are and what you see, there is no you, there is no it; there is no observer, there is no observed. There is no seen and there is no seer; there is no lover and there is no beloved. There is only *what is*. *What is* is a dynamic force. It's ongoing — a journey without end. When you see it, you are that journey.

* * *

23 *July* 1979

Who can enquire, who can look at something directly, is someone who needs to see the reality whatever the consequence; someone whose need to love is so great that they are no longer interested in collecting another romance; someone whose yearning for God is so intense that they're not going to take another structure, another form upon their shoulders to weigh themselves down. They're intensely interested, they're sharp; every nerve, every cell, is longing to understand.

When people say "I look at it, but it doesn't change", what does it mean? Are you looking with that quality? Because it's not a question of it changing; when you look with that intensity, you're changing — you're transforming, you're vibrating at that wavelength yourself. It must respond. That response to the intensity is the merger; that's the softness, that's the love, that's the light, and it takes you deeper into itself. At that point it's choiceless awareness — the journey is without choice. Everything that you do in your life at that point is meditation. The very fact of living teaches you more, unfolds, goes deeper — in the simplest ways. You see a face, you see a form, you see anything; it introduces you to the depth of love, of life. There's no 'how to' in that place, there's no 'what if' in that place, there's no 'should I' in that place, there's no 'why me' in that place. There's no question — because nothing is hidden. For one who needs to love, nothing is hidden.

Any time that you feel a great yearning or need, that is the time that you can see this dimension. Until that moment you cannot bring it about, you cannot invent it, you cannot do any of these things. And there's no need to — if you've just had a glimpse of it, you understand, you know it waits for you; you know it also yearns for you now, but it cannot do anything. That space, that vastness is without power; it simply waits. Once you've had a glimpse of it, you won't be able to live without it. It's a question of time. The very request, the very energy, the very question is responded to, and the answer will never be more than the question allows. You'll only experience the love that you're able to receive. So if you feel there's a lack in your life, you'll understand why — the preparation is limited.

Questioner: Are you saying that if someone is lonely they're unprepared?

Daniel: Go deeper now. Your longing has introduced you to something, but it has not fulfilled it. So that non-fulfillment indicates that you need to go a bit further now; the preparation isn't enough. You may just need a physical preparation around you, you may need to develop some health now, physical health. You may need to create a circumstance where the family is no longer dependent on you. You may need to find a language that allows you to facilitate that movement. So what's happening is that a refinement is taking place. As you understand your own need to love, deeply, how can you live without it? Once you're touching it, it's calling you.

24 July 1979

* * *

Stillness is not an energy which precludes sound or movement. I would say that stillness is a sense of order; where there is no chaos, where you can perceive that the universe is relationship. And you can only see it when you're related to it yourself. That capacity to perceive the essential relationships in life, I would say, is stillness.

Before we can come upon this quality of stillness, obviously we have to understand what is happening around us. Heretofore we've tried to understand what's happening around us by describing it. I find personally that the description is not the fact; that my description of life is removed from the fact. I've found that you can understand what's going on around you by your response to it, by your feelings. When you see something and you feel pain, that pain introduces you to yourself. That to me is the point of perception — the doorway to perception. When I understand that outwardly, the effect is inward — I see something, and I feel; I see something, and I react; I see something, and I respond. In that, I come to understand that I'm intimately connected to what I experience and see. Without the understanding of that center called 'me', what I see outwardly is limited. When I understand the intimate connection, I've now embarked on a journey. Anytime I attempt to leave that journey prematurely, I'll again know pain.

The journey is to love, the journey is to fulfillment. There's no end.

5 August 1979

* * *

Mystery is the distance that we put between ourselves and love, between ourselves and God, between ourselves and the universe. We have kept it mysterious in order not to realize it.

It is not unavailable; first-hand contact is not unavailable. But through borrowed philosophy we let ourselves off the hook. I have no argument with the statements made by great and wise people who have felt a need to understand life. All they say to me is that there is a yearning — there has always been a yearning to touch divinity, to touch fullness.

5 August 1979

* * *

There are words to express it, but the actual silence is the only communication. We can go as far with the word as necessary, but when the word is no longer necessary, then a certain stillness may prevail.

6 August 1979

* * *

Relationship, actual relationship, is when there is no separation. Then all like energies move toward the essence. Always, when there is no imposed condition, life moves to the essence.

7 August 1979

* * *

In simply being, you're moving to an essence — that's what waiting is.

7 August 1979

* * *

Understanding is the essential discovery that you don't really know. That discovering is the receptivity that allows love to flower.

16 August 1979

* * *

You may see that you have put together a relationship or a marriage out of pressure, or fears, or loneliness, or whatever — you may recognize that it was created by you — without your effort, the likelihood of it happening didn't seem great. You recognize that your marriage, or whatever you've done, you've put together for some reason, and this reason has come out of the past. In that you recognize that the relationship which you have contrived or formulated has rough edges. It is your creation, and your creation is like you. It looks the other way, it knows when to avoid, it seeks pleasure, it can deceive itself, it does so many things; and you see it, and you're in it. The very seeing of it, the very seeing of your capacity to deceive yourself and understanding the ramifications of that self-deception, introduces you to a great care. So you may have invented or developed a marriage through your own manipulations and pressures, but now you're no longer pressured, you're no longer manipulating; now you're no longer creating it through effort, because you see the ramifications of that activity.

In that, you're able to simply look at it, see its quality, and feel what it is. Can it stand without your support structure? Does it have a vital quality without your anxiety — do you constantly need to juggle it, or does it have a quality of its own? When you need to live a life of quality, when you need to live a life that no longer has mediocrity in it, then you're able to look at whatever you've created with that interest, that real eagerness, that understanding. When you can look at what you've created with that eagerness, without interfering with it, it will speak to you. It will indicate its quality.

The relationship must stand on its own. A relationship that only exists with a support structure, only exists in sacrifice and pressures and fears, is only a relationship of torment, not a relationship of freedom or understanding. If freedom and understanding is essential to you, then it will also be essential that it is inherent in everything you do. So although the first step may be contrived, before the second step, you've woken up. In waking up, you've introduced light into relationship. You've recognized your need; you realize the need that whatever you do must be true, must be full. And you also realize that you cannot invent truth, you can simply recognize it — and when you're eager to do so, you will recognize it. When you're no longer asserting yourself in the society around you, when you're no longer concocting your dreams, my feeling is that the reality you see is much vaster than any dream, any formula that you can come up with. The fact of creation does not need imitation; the fact of creation is so much vaster than your manipulation. So real creativity is to let the creation speak through you. Real health is simply not to impose a condition of sickness upon ourselves. And real relationship is to see, in freedom, the obvious interrelation of all things in this universe.

* * *

28 August 1979

In the last few years, we have built quite a mystique around this word enlightenment. To me it just means to turn the light on, so that things become clear. You turn the light on in yourself and it is clear why you exist, what you are about, what you are doing. And when the light is on inside of yourself, the light is also on outside; you see a harmonious relationship with *what is*.

Health is to be fully absorbed in what you are doing. The absence of that absorption I would call illness — any time that one is not living fully, there is separation — separation between the essence and the expression. That separation leaves room for illness, or disability, or tragedy, or disaster of one sort or another.

* * *

5 September 1979

When the heart is not speaking, you'll adopt psychological guidelines. When you see clearly, then you're no longer pressured; when you don't see clearly, then you borrow opinion. When the heart does not speak, the mind speaks. When a person can't *see*, then thought takes over. When the community cannot function, government organizes. So anytime there is no real understanding, anytime the expression is so far removed from the essence, then in that space thought enters, history enters, guidelines enter; suppression, repression, expression all enter in there. So we take on the guidelines, and we have imposed guidelines upon ourselves, because a quality of life does not express itself, has not blossomed. So when there are too many guidelines, there's an indication that intelligence is lacking.

As we move through life we have an effect. And these effects can be scars; or one can move through life without creating any scars at all. So it's really to understand the need; again and again and again it comes back to that — to understand the need. Do you understand the need in your life?

Questioner: No, I don't understand the need in my life.

Daniel: So that's the stuff of meditation — to look around and see what has happened, to look around and see the effect of society, the effect of just living. One may understand that there's a need for a quality of freshness and vitality in life.

Questioner: We are getting married, and a baby is expected soon. We may start traveling around the country on our way to California.

Daniel: You know, I'm very concerned with these new marriages. The potential for newness is there. And when that potential for newness is there, it has a sacred quality — a softness. That softness needs preparation and stability. One prepares to live a life without fear. When the societal structure is not in order, it threatens. It's very important in life that you come to a point where you're not living in fear. And by that I don't mean to be oblivious; I mean that it's all taken care of — there's a home, there are savings, the basic needs are provided for. So, if that's possible, even if you can't physically do it at the moment, you can recognize the need that you and yours don't live in fear. And if you can come to that yourself physically, then you'll find the ability to provide for others who are also in need.

Are your parents alive? Do they get frightened when you tell them your plans?

Q: Yes.

Daniel: Then you have to provide for that family also. They're not incorrect, you know. It sounds so conservative, but they're not incorrect. When something is imbalanced, the old folks are a good barometer. Maybe what they're saying is not exactly correct or true, but their disturbance or their fear indicates something — because there's a great inner pressure in every parent that the children find security. Now the security they know may be stultifying — a good job, money in the bank, or whatever. So either demonstrate that you have that, or demonstrate that you don't need it. But if you don't demonstrate a quality of intelligence or a wellbeing that they can perceive, they'll live in fear for you, and the relationship will never be balanced until this is reconciled.

One of the great needs in relationship to family is that they can live their life in peace; I'm no longer presenting a difficulty to them. The only way it can happen is that I'm actually living my life in peace, and that they are able to live their life in peace. But if I'm constantly in difficulties, then I can't convince them that they shouldn't be worried about me — they'll be worried. So I discover that my real peace is also their peace — meaning that I'm no longer creating a problem for them in their lives. A great need in parents is that their children come to peace, come to fullness. It's all connected. To understand that basic connection — where you come from is also what you'll be creating. So the condition you had with your father, be prepared to have with your child.

But if in the middle of that past and future, the present, you find a quality that is eternal — you're no longer bound by the historical process. Touching on that dimension in your life is also to give birth to something fresh and vital — whether it's a baby, or understanding, it's one and the same. Having found that peace, the child may be born in peace. Most of us have had a situation in the past where we were not born in peace; we were born in projection, we were born in so many ideas, we were born in hopes, schemes, dreams — all projected into the future around the child. And that projection can really create havoc for the child. But a child that's born in actual love, fullness, understanding, *is* a product of that understanding. Then you have a family that's growing together, that's learning together.

9 September 1979

* * *

Questioner: There seems to be a fear that comes as one ages.

Daniel: When you get frightened you may start reacting, or try to change that process, or get away from it, or overcome it — or become oblivious to it, or whatever. And when you get frightened or you react to it, it seems to work in reverse — when you get frightened, the very fear makes you look older, in fact accelerates the aging process. It would be my feeling that any time you think that you are a child, or an adolescent, or a senior citizen or whatever, you are susceptible to the pressures of that time period. Do you remember the pressures you felt as a teenager? In retrospect they seem like carefree years, but in those years they weren't so carefree; they were really competitive, pressure filled, fearful — not very different than the adult years.

Questioner: I think they were worse.

Daniel: They may have been worse. My feeling is that we have never lived fully — we've never experienced life. What we have experienced is the possibility of living; that there is a potential in each of us to live. And what we have called life is not life at all, it's just memory. What we have called birth is not birth; birth only takes place when a being has touched this quality of life, when he or she is living fully in their potential, when they're no longer stuck in time. We have called this measurement life; but to me life is not bound in time. Only when one has realized a life that is not bound in time can we actually say that one is alive fully, one is a human being. So the childhood we mourn for, the adolescence that we long for, and the old age that we're frightened of, are only our memory, only our illusion, our invention. As long as you live within that creation and illusion, you'll have to know pressure and fear. What we mourn for is our memory, not the fact.

Fullness in life is not this historical process. Full life is a new dimension, a new clarity — a being that is unfettered, that is not limited. That being does not fear old age or death, or anything, because that being can see clearly. Being alive, he or she can see life, and no longer lives in fear. And I would say that each of us is a potential human being. We have the potential to be fully human. We have the potential to be free. And if one realizes that need, it must come. For a human being who discovers the need, who understands the need to live fully and clearly — not bound by these psychic states and pressures — to realize the need is to touch a human quality in life. To realize this need is also to touch a divine quality. Because when you realize the need to be free, you've also realized the need to touch God, to be in love. When you realize the need, you've introduced light into your life, you've turned the light on. In simply realizing the need to be a full human being — to live a full life — in that moment you've just developed receptivity.

When you yearn to love, when you yearn to merge, when you yearn for a universal quality, you've also come to realize in that moment the limitation of what is man-made. When that yearning is taking place, when one has touched on stillness, in that moment something vital is born. The moment you understand, the moment you can see, the moment you can feel fully, is the moment that you can say you're actually born, that life begins. And that life knows no fear and no mourning, and no projection. When you in fact are born, when you in fact are alive, then what you give birth to is also free, is also new.

* * *
9 September 1979

To me there are qualities of tension, or degrees of tension. Now, I would say that when you project a future goal, the distance between yourself and that goal would be tension. Now you can see it in the simplest physical way; when it's raining, or it's cold, and you're walking home, and you have half a mile to go or whatever, you can't wait to get home. That distance between the goal and yourself is what you would call tension and pressure. So that tension that exists in a projected goal, in the movement through time and space, is what we would call a psychological tension. You posit something outside of yourself to attain or to achieve. Once you've posited *there*, and you've made that *there* necessary, not being there would be the stuff of tension. Not having what you've projected would be the stuff of psychological pressure — whatever it is.

The very desire, without the actual having, will be the stuff of tension. In this social existence, there may be a great pressure and tension — fear of not having, fear of loss, fear of loneliness; fear of not having a mate, fear of being stuck with a mate forever; fear of not having any money, fear of having too much money and having it stolen; fear of being disliked, or liked for the wrong reason. These are the forms of psychological tension and pressure. And now there's also something that is called creative tension. In order to write, in order to paint, you may need to create or generate tension as a constant. You may need to go around town or into the city to acquire subject matter. Much of what we call art nowadays is something that is produced from this so-called creative tension, this pressure. It's a sort of whipping oneself, a kind of stimulation.

But now as I enquire deeper into the whole subject matter of tension, I find that even on the psychological level, tension indicates an absence, a lack, an imbalance. And I examine it — is it that there is a lack of money, is it that there is a lack of shelter, is there a lack of food, is there a lack of community? And I see that these things aren't lacking, that there is enough; that physically I may have established a security; everything is in working order, I'm not dependent on anything. Socially everything is taken care of; and I still detect what I call tension. Then I ask, what is lacking? What's the source of this tension now, if socially everything is in order? And with that I start to probe deeper. Because the first expression to me still seems to be correct. Originally tension to me was that something was out there; the space between myself and that 'thereness', that goal, that projected goal, I felt to be tension. Now all the social and psychological goals I had, I've experienced; and I have a basic security, a social and physical security. And yet the tension exists. At that moment I discover that what I'm calling tension is still a separation; but it has a different quality now — it's not a separation from anything that I know.

And now I come to understand that what I called tension and pressure is a signal that indicates to me the division within myself, the conflict within myself. In short, I make a discovery that this tension is an indication that I have not reached, and am not living in, my fullest potential. That tension indicates to me that I've imposed a limitation upon myself; that I have not realized or experienced the purpose of life, the meaning of life; there's some lack somewhere. When I experience what I call that lack, I also come to experience the need. When I know that I cannot fill that lack with anything known, with any acquisition — and yet that separation is very real to me — I experience a great need in my life. Then what is called tension and pressure comes to serve as a guideline, a signal — the invitation to go deeper. Tension is an invitation, pressure is an invitation.

Questioner: It seems to me that identity, or just the feeling of self, when looked at, very often is tension itself — that I am tension. It seems as though there are energies, polarities actually feeding into each other constantly; they're wired into each other — opposing energies that form the ego through thought.

Daniel: Any time that you have constructed a center, or crystallized an ego-structure called 'I', then it will have its opposite. What is actually the separation from here to there? Here is 'me' as the center, and there is outside of me. The very structure of the center called 'me' will be tension. So that to me is the essential tension — that I am in the way of merger. The way I am — what I think, what I want, what I do — my activity in fact is the sickness, is the illness, is the tension, is the impediment. I am here, and the world is outside. And I'm trying to reconcile the outside world without understanding that I've created the outside world — through my stance, through my position — and now I'm trying to deal with it. So, when I experience tension, I also experience myself. That tension again serves as a signal of this separation.

I get a glimpse that all of this is miraculous — the very fact of rain beating on the leaves, the very fact that a hand moves, the very fact that I can feel and move; I get a glimpse at times that it's all vast, that it's all moving. And none of it appears to be thought-constructed, dependent on anyone's ability to think it up. The harmony, the interrelationship of the universe seems to be a fact; it can be appreciated. And when I look at myself, it also seems to be a marvel of coordination; the very working of the body, and how it moves through space, seems to be a marvel. But then an incident takes place, and it is gone. What happened to the marvel of a moment ago? So I see that this so-called marvel is dependent on certain things. My capacity to see the marvelous — my capacity to see the relationships that exist in this universe — came in fact from the absence of 'me' as a dominating center.

So I see that 'me' arises only under certain conditions. When everything is at peace, and when there's no psychological pressure on me, then I can appreciate the interrelationships in this universe; I am part of it. But when I meet another psyche, another psychological condition, another center, these centers polarize. That polarization is space, distance, time. So it's only in relationship that I'm confronted with this tension, pressure, and fear. The fact of the universe may be relationship and harmony; but the capacity to recognize that fact requires a human being who has no impediments to that recognition.

14 September 1979

* * *

When one sees the light at the end of the tunnel, there is an irresistible urgency to merge with it, to experience it. That is what is meant by yearning. When you glimpse this light, you yearn for it. All things yearn to merge with this essence or source of energy.

And that movement towards merger is a journey of light. Life only takes place when that yearning is there, when that attraction is there. Then the movement towards the light is a movement in consciousness. The perception of light is an awakening of consciousness, and the yearning to merge with that light is a journey in consciousness.

18 September 1979

* * *

When you are in conflict in your life, you are usually met with the very situation that will point out the limitation in your lifestyle. That situation is an exact response to what you are; it is the situation that you need most to wake up in your life. Life is always that movement to wake up; there's always that opportunity to awaken. So we may imagine a life or want a life without difficulty, without pain; but that life is not the life we need. The life that we need is the life that we've created, which in fact tells us what we are. The life we've created is the actual mirror that will allow us to see what we're doing. It seems to be quite finely tuned. All the movement, everything that we've created, is done almost with precision. We create the very thing that generates the most sorrow and pain. It's almost as if we've calculated, done everything in this life to bring on that hurt; to make that hurt so intense in our lives that there is no choice — but to realize the need for love, to realize the need for God.

23 September 1979

* * *

In this exploration, one awakens to the fact, the simple fact, that you're loved — that's all, you just realize that you're loved. You see how blended it all is, how intricate it all is, how perfect it all is, how interrelated it all is. You see it, you actually see it. And in seeing the intricate relationships that exist in this life, and how balanced it all is, you recognize that you're immersed in love. Until that moment, you were preoccupied with your affairs and ideas and schemes and dreams and hopes — and in that one moment when you're not preoccupied with self, you see the immensity. In that moment you awaken to the fact that you're sitting in the middle of love — you're right in the middle of it — and it's not personal. It's anonymous — it hasn't made any claim on you; it's an unconditional love and you recognize it. You see — how shall I put it — you see that you're bathed in light, you see that you're immersed in love, and always have been. But it's only in that minute that you've recognized it. You recognize God's grace, and that's it's unconditional. When you recognize that quality, life is changed for you; a quality emerges. When you experience God's love, a similar quality unfolds in you; and as that unfolding takes place, there's a response to God's love, there's a response to this light — there's a great need to immerse yourself in it, there's a great need to merge with it. When you experience God's love, without any demand on you, you feel the great need to be lovely. You feel the need to be excellent. And by excellent I do not mean a perfectionistic attitude. It's not an attitude, but the very ending of the center; it is the ending of the 'me', the surrendering of opinions and information. So a response to God's love is surrender in the face of it.

Now this word God has been so bound in the past years that it's difficult to hear it in its pure state. The reason I'm utilizing it now is because we have spent this last few months moving along together, and most of us have through our presence here formulated an agreement to see, to experience. So we're moving in an ongoing exploration. It is not dependent on this place; this exploration will carry on wherever we go. But in moving together, we can come to a point where we experience that what we've always been seeking, what we've been looking for — we're in fact standing in the middle of it, and we always have been right in the midst of it. And one only experiences this when one has seen the limitation in the seeking — that in fact when you are seeking, you are preceded by your information, which creates a screen around you. You cannot see the simplicity; all you see is what you project. When you are so bound, when you feel the tremendous burden you put on yourself, when you constantly run into walls you create, you make a discovery of the prison you walk in, that you create around yourself.

When that prison is intolerable, you yearn; you realize a need to see a quality not bound by thought, not bound in time and space. You awaken to the need to touch reality, something real. In that yearning to touch something real, one experiences what I can call a quality of light or divinity. A stillness is there — in the yearning to touch something real you experience a stillness, and in seeing that stillness you experience what I could call God's grace. It is unconditional — whatever you've done, whoever you are, whatever you've thought of yourself; whatever sin, crime or absurdity you've committed — in that moment of stillness there's no such thing. So when one awakens to God's grace, one awakens to the fact that one is in the midst of this energy. And the awakening to that indicates that this quality exists in you. That quality in you yearns to unite, yearns to merge. God's love arouses in you a feeling to be lovely. That to me is marriage, that to me is relationship. When loveliness and love merge, something new, something vital, something fresh is born.

29 September 1979

* * *

Only when one recognizes love in its purest state, and merges with that love, has one touched reality. Only then does your art become reality; only then does your relationship, your marriage, whatever you've created, become vital. Having touched this essence, the essence expresses itself through the action. The activity divorced from essence contributes nothing to this life. The essential need, the great need in life is to touch, to merge with the source; to touch the essence, to merge with it. The great need is to love so fully that the entire body, the entire being is transformed. That transformed quality is transforming — to everything it touches.

When a being with that vitality, with that vital quality, meets another being in that intensity, what is that marriage like; and what is the end product of that marriage, what is the baby that comes out of that marriage? In Hindu mythology there are many stories of Shiva and Shakti, locked in a love embrace for thousands of years. She was the eternal virgin, even though from the moment they met they were making love, and he was the eternal celibate. In the midst of their lovemaking they maintained purity. The parallel I make to that story is that to me, lovemaking is that — lovemaking is full only when virginity and celibacy is experienced. And I do not mean a stance, or any form of behavior. When the love is so deep, and so intense, there are no scars in it, there's no memory of the act. And when the love is so great that there is no residue, no memory of the action taking place, I would say that the child is conceived without memory, without prior conditioning — whether that child is actually the form called child, or is actually something new that comes out of the relationship. To me, the child or the infant is just a manifestation of that love. It may take the form of an infant, but the manifestation of that love can happen in so many ways.

A quality like that is the need. And if it's the need it must happen. If you can perceive what we were just discussing — actually perceive it — what stands in the way? If one is not preoccupied with their thought and their ideas, then one may recognize God's love — simply put. In seeing the fineness, in experiencing the intricacy, one yearns to merge with it, to experience it even further.

Questioner: *I feel empty of questions. It seems that waiting is just enough.*

Daniel: But waiting must be a dynamic; and to wait means that the basic issue is resolved. To wait means that you've recognized what must be. The basis of waiting is the recognition of *what is.* When you can see and experience *what is,* you also see in that moment what must be. Then each action that takes place, from that moment on, is a universal action, is a divine action.

So it's ironic — what we are saying now sounds very much like religious scripture. So one may come to a point where one can realize scripture, make scripture, experience scripture directly. In feeling that quality, that scripture lives in you.

29 September 1979

II. DISCUSSIONS AND DEEPER ENQUIRIES

This section consists of exchanges and conversations in Ithaca and Woodstock. The interview format was used experimentally to allow a deeper exploration of the subject matter.

Introduction

Daniel: We're starting from a premise — that a heartfelt question, a question expressed with intensity, is not merely a question; but actually a deep, intensified expression of yearning. That quality, that intensity in fact is the creator of the answer; it creates the response. So to my mind, the question that comes from deep inside one enlightens. It's not the answer that enlightens; but in fact the question which sheds light upon the subject. The intensity of the question illustrates the need. When the need is bared, when the need is exposed, when the need is revealed — the answer is the response. So the question in fact indicates the degree of receptivity. Obviously when the question is so intense, the receptivity is so deep, then the answer will also have this penetrating force.

I've likened it in the past to the question being the passion, and the answer being the essence that responds to that passion. When question and answer merge, we can say that something new, fresh and vital has taken place. When the interviewer understands that in fact he is not simply interviewing, but is discovering, transforming — then the interviewer and the interviewed are moving in conjunction, moving in cooperation. They both perceive the need. That is the generating or creative quality that I'm referring to as an interview. Heretofore the interview form has not allowed that to take place. We may have touched it, approached it. But it seems now that the need is great — can the interview allow us to make a breakthrough?

There is a premise, and an affection is established; and so the questioning must also have the understanding that the capacity to touch the deepest, the fullest, is here.

14 August 1979

The Responsibility of Communication

Daniel: First, before we ask a question, can we see if it is coming from deep within us, if it is a basic question to us? If you feel that the question is essential, then can you meditate on it deeply, can you refine it and verbalize it in a concise way? If you have done that basic work, the very question is a dynamic that seeks its answer, that finds its answer. This finding of the correct question is energy, and then the expression of the question is energy. The full question, finding the correct answer, is a love affair — it's a marriage, it's a merger, it's a surrender. And in that moment of surrender you're opened up to something beyond you. When the question has clarified itself, has purified itself so that it is essence, it finds within itself the answer.

So the first question, which you brought up earlier today, was what is this observer? Unless you really meet this entity called the observer and know it intimately, you're approaching life through a lens, through a construct, having the impression that you know; and you're never really coming in contact with anything. The observer is 'me' — my wants, my hopes, my dreams, my information. It thinks that what it sees is outside itself. But this 'me' only sees what it is. It does not see anything outside of itself actually, but it gets a glimpse of something outward, and what it sees in that split second, it names. That name comes from its own information bank, its own background. When it sees someone that it's met before, it doesn't see this person, it sees its information about that person; it sees the past. So this so-called observer or 'me' is living in its own little world. It makes no contact with itself and it makes no contact with the environment or the universe. When this 'me' or observer is introduced time and time again to the fact that everything that it is looking at is in actuality its own information, then it is forced to look at the source of that information. And when its forced to look at the source of the information there is no such thing as the observed any longer. There is only the observer.

When the observer is no longer focusing all its energy on the outer circumstance, but looks at itself with that intensity, it is now turned inward to see its own nature. When this observer views itself, it undergoes a change. As long as the construct existed of observer and observed, they went together; but when you realize that what you see is what you are, there is no longer an observed — and hence no longer an observer. Now when we go deeper into it and we're left with neither observed nor observer, there's a different world, a different universe. When there is no 'me' to separate the outer and the inner, then you understand that no separation exists.

Steven: So in meditation one may come to that point.

Daniel: But we must realize that point — not just as some theory. We've come to have the impression that we know what so many books or speakers are saying, and therefore we don't actually experience it. What does it mean when there's no separation between the outer and the inner? Not through any hypnotized state, not through any belief system, but what does it mean when I perceive that essentially there is no difference between you and myself — 'me' and 'you' do not exist? What happens in your life when you perceive that?

Very much like a child you learn to move. You have to look around; you're in a world you don't know. And so now understanding has a different quality to it; it's not an intellectual understanding, it's an understanding that happens inwardly, outwardly, all around you. If something is hurt outside of you it's very much like a wound on you, in your body. The pain, the happiness, the health and the ill health around you is also what you feel inside yourself. And again, it is not coming out of hypnosis or through any pressure; you are recognizing it.

Yet one is able to be the identity, as well as to put the identity aside. One is able to have a functional separation, that uses 'me' and 'you' when it's necessary; but one also still has the fundamental perception that 'me' and 'you' is a convenience, not a fact to be constantly reinforced. So before one can love, before one can feel, before one can marry, one must come to this understanding of no separation — this stillness. All expression that takes place while division still exists is self-perpetuation.

So see what you're feeling now. When the mind is thrown back on itself, it starts to understand that something is happening other than its own problems, its own desires, its own wants, its own constructs. Then life has a certain sacred quality; it's not to be treated so lightly. When you understand that everything you express has an effect, and you see how vast and unending the effect can be, then what you say and what you do has a different quality to it.

S: *It seems, from what I can hear, that there is not an enlightenment, but there may be a movement away from conditioning toward freedom.*

Daniel: There's a realization that you're enlightened already, but you've been acting in a very unenlightened way, that's all. You've been saying things and not living by them, acting a certain way and not feeling or understanding the ramifications. And because you're saying things without understanding them, there's sorrow in your life.

So then we come to the next stage. Can this understanding that we've had be manifested on earth? Can this energy, this stillness that you feel in your life manifest around you now? Because if your environment does not also feel the stillness — if the community you're living in is not particpating in or partaking of this stillness — then you have to seriously question the depth of the state that you're in. Through understanding of the observer and the observed, you may be introduced to a fundamental state called silence or personal freedom. You see how it all works, you're not constricted by the social scene or the social situation any longer, and there's no problem for you. But the evidence at hand is that there is a problem for the rest of the world. Once you feel this silence, this state of freedom, you have a responsibility to find a way to communicate it. You may not feel any separation from the environment, from the universe, but you may be talking to beings who are conditioned to believe that this separation exists. Communication can take place only in the thorough absence of 'you'. When this absence or silence is so great in you, then you see what the other's need is rather than what you would like for them. Then your response is not based on your idea, but is a real expression of this love or compassion through understanding the need. And you can only do that when you are the other person; when you've perceived them to such an extent that there's no separation.

So you may see that there's no separation between body, thought and the unconscious — they're just words, just constructs. But you're also living in a society of people who feel that there is a separation. In order to communicate, we may have to go step by step. And in going step by step we may discover that there is no separation. That mutual discovery is the important thing. Without that mutual discovery, what takes place is suggestion or domination or force or pressure, and everything that the other person is experiencing is only temporary or limited; it is not coming from a full understanding. When you see that you and the society around you are one and the same, and you must relate to that society, then you have to find a way. You are the one responsible. The communication is your responsibility because you've touched on something.

S: *Can everyone find this silence?*

Daniel: I say, "I love you". Can everyone hear that in its pure state? Or will everyone take that statement to mean what they want it to mean? My feeling is that very few will understand "I love you", will hear it to mean exactly what it means. But people who hear "I love you" will hear it to mean what they'd like to to mean, what they're conditioned to hope it means. It's only the being that has that intensity, that's moving in the same quality with you, who is going to hear it in its purest state — with the absence of entity, usage and manipulation. But if most beings are involved to some extent in continuity and self-perpetuation, then they're going to hear "I love you" as part of that.

So you must understand to whom you're talking, and the effect it will have. It becomes very important not to push people into a situation that is not true for their present circumstance. If you are fixed in the idea that this basic understanding or full realization is necessary for everyone, then you may not be able to see the person in front of you, and what their needs are. Communication is your responsibility — to see what the need is, again and again and again. Disturbance in the relationships around you will indicate the lack of communication. All violence comes out of lack of communication.

There is an energy in this life that's vast; it can be called God, or love, or whatever name you choose. And each life form must someday recognize its oneness with that energy, with this universe, with God — must feel love if it is to carry on. But the realization of that need comes to different people at different times, in different ways. If you try to force that realization, or create some construct where that will be realized, it is not a full realization. Only one who has recognized his full need is ready to hear it, is ready to breathe it, is ready to participate in it fully.

There are some along the way who are finding out that everything they cling to or hope for is not supporting them or fulfilling them. That non-fulfillment is pointing to something. Everyone needs to love, but very few people have felt this need so thoroughly that they will not accept substitution or an artificial circumstance. Most will have to go through many forms before this realization can take place. There is no higher or lower, no hierarchy in that. A person who realizes his need at twelve years old is not higher than a person who realizes it at eighty years old. One who is doing mantras is not higher or lower than a person who perceives God simply, as a fact in his life. What's your capacity, what's your need? What is the challenge? In recognizing the challenge and the need, the way is clear. If you're not in touch with the need, and if you can't formulate it, then the way is confused.

S: *Then what is the role of techniques?*

Daniel: If we've been moving together thus far, you can understand that techniques, just like the statement "I love you", can only be understood and utilized by someone who is free — free from ego, free from entity, free of desire, free of wants, free of pleasure, free of fear. One who has made contact with this fundamental energy, and feels it inside and outside of himself — in short, one who has seen God — is one who can therefore apply everything around him, not for self-perpetuation, but to manifest peace and love in this life. For one who has not touched fullness, who is living within the confines of ego, this phrase "I love you" becomes a powerful phrase that can be quite violent — it becomes a weapon. But to a being who is not bound by ego, this phrase "I love you" can express an energy of togetherness — of sharing, of feeling.

In the past, the guru saw the needs of the disciple and initiated him in the technique that was applicable to him at that time. So the mantra was really an expression of their relationship, an exchange of energy between guru and disciple — between lovers. But now these techniques, used by someone who is not clear, who does not understand what his needs are and who he is, become instruments of further division. A being who realizes his need and what he's about, who is not violent to himself or others around him, can then see these techniques, these mantras, these forms, and see where they apply and where they don't apply. He can experiment with them also. You can experiment with various forms of so-called healing as long as this contact with these psychic forces through techniques is not personalized. Then what is the harm — explore everything, look at everything; why be afraid of anything? The idea that gurus and techniques are bad becomes nonsense, a waste of energy. There's nothing bad or good; everything can have fullness and realization or bondage in it, depending on the doer. But if you're trying to find love or relationship or God through chanting or mantras, or through any of these so-called sensitivity courses, then my feeling is that there's a basic limitation. A modification of behavior can take place with these techniques, but a feeling of completeness does not come out of a modification of behavior. Love or oneness with the universe is not modification of behavior. The need is not to overcome the intellect, but to integrate it.

First make contact, first invite this energy into your being; first feel, first see what's going on around you. Then when you've familiarized yourself with this energy and you have the need to go further, healing may be something you see to be necessary and therefore you manifest. Many beings in the past have made contact with this energy, have come to some point of understanding, and are satisfied with that state; but the challenge is a bit different now — it's not only to make contact with this energy but to manifest it, to demonstrate it. The need around us is great — the need is for the general level of mankind's recognition to expand. We can't make little nations or sects of our own and think of ourselves as higher or more advanced; it's silly, and it also perpetuates the separation and violence. The next step is to have the responsibility to share it, because you have a need to communicate and share it. If there is a failure in communication, the failure is ours, not the other person's. Find a way. And in finding a way, techniques may be useful. First feel this immensity, and then demonstrate it. But if you attempt to demonstrate it without feeling, you will only create more heartbreak.

S: So in other words, wait until it's totally clear?

Daniel: You have no choice. First feel it, and then it will move you. But we must not stop at that point; we must go deeper. As you're finding a way, you're also refining yourself, you're going deeper in this energy.

When you come to a point through any technique where you are now ready to look, you must also understand when to put that technique aside. A being who needs to look at life and needs to understand it will look at anything; and part of this discovery is to discover the so-called unconscious or psychic forces, to understand what they are. Part of this discovery is to understand the nature of vibrations and sound, and their effect on the body and on the environment. Very much a part of this discovery is to understand all the techniques and approaches that mankind has devised to make contact with something greater than himself. Further exploration is to understand the nature of the symbols that humankind has used to express its longing. There may be many corrupt forms around us, but the forms are indicating that there is some need. I'm not doubting the corruption that has taken place around these techniques and forms, but to negate it is also to be insensitive. I don't mean that one should go after these forms or elevate them, but I would say that as a sensitive being it is your responsibility to understand why they exist in the first place — why romance exists, why these approaches exist — to understand humankind's need to make contact with the universal. When you do recognize that it's not the way, make sure you don't destroy anything in the process — just realize that it's not the way.

So we've come in this enquiry to this point — we're asking people who have come and shared with us closely, can you make this contact, can you feel it? Can you put aside this observer and observed, and the negative approach, and the positive approach — can you just feel? First you must feel; then we can investigate. Then we can see the negative approach and the positive approach, then we can understand all the approaches. But first let's feel, that's the basis of our relationship; that fundamental affection is necessary. Because if you don't have that fundamental feeling, if you don't make that contact, you won't be able to contain the discovery.

8 August 1978

The Communication of Freedom

Steven: Could we look further at how it is possible to communicate a sense of freedom, understanding, or enlightenment?

Daniel: If you come to what you call freedom or a sense of quiet, and the circumstance around you is not equally free and quiet, at that point you have to question your freedom — is there something you're overlooking? Why are you not able to communicate this quiet, this freedom and this peace in such a way that the environment and the people around you are also participating in it fully? The responsibility is yours. The individual's so-called peace and freedom is lacking if the society around him is involved in war and hurt.

So you must find out why what you're feeling is not being transmitted, why it's not being conveyed. Having come to a point of what feels like fulfillment, I see that it's not full — not because I lack anything that I can see, but because I see the oneness with humanity around me, and it's in pain. Aspects of yourself are in pain. Now your work must go deeper, you must go further in understanding. When I think I am this body, then this body's pain is my pain, and I can't separate myself from it. I must understand my body and it must be in good health. And now if I make contact with the larger body of mankind, then its pain is also my pain. I can't be oblivious to it, or use my realization to create a separate state. So if there is something imbalanced outwardly, it's indicating that there's more work to do, there's deeper to go. Find a way.

S: Okay, but missionaries aren't the answer.

The Communication of Freedom   85

Daniel: Missionary work is not what I'm talking about. Missionary work is usually based on reward or punishment, attracting someone with rewards of heaven, or the promise of a better life. It is a new value system in which behavior can be modified, but it is not coming out of perception or change.

S: Okay — *then in opposition to the idea of missionaries is the idea of saving the world through saving oneself.*

Daniel: It's not saving the world, it's understanding yourself. When you have this idea of saving the world, you're already doomed, because then *you* saving the world is you saving something outside of yourself — how is it separate from you that you're going to save it? So you're not saving the world, you're going deeper into yourself. As you see the pain and the hurt around you, you're researching, you're finding a way to communicate. The pain around you is just a lack of communication. Research the past and see if there's a way to communicate; find out who you are, look around you. If you have that quality and that intensity, then a way is there. This need to communicate is such a dynamic that a purification is going on. You see how you're sharpening yourself in this process. As you're going deeper and deeper into it, you're refining yourself, and your capacity to feel is even greater. So it's your further realization that we're talking about, not saving the world.

S: *There's an immediate tendency to concretize what you're saying.*

Daniel: Then the concretization will collapse. There will be cracks through time, and it will fall apart, just like many other organizations and support systems have fallen apart. The only reason a support system exists is because something can't stand on its own.

S: *Is there any way to directly communicate without the concretization coming into play?*

Daniel: Full communication takes place between beings whose hearts are open. Communication may be to never say a word. To some, communication may be what is called physical absence. To some, communication may be a hug or an embrace or a touch. But if that touch is given to the wrong person, it's not communication, it's separation. Then you must be careful that these hugs or words are not misunderstood. You have the spectrum of communication available to you. See what applies. You'll make mistakes, and through these mistakes you'll learn. As long as there's no motive for self-perpetuation, these mistakes will not be irreparable. But if this becomes a process of self-aggrandizement, then the scars will be deep — even though it's in the name of so-called help or care.

So when we come together as a community we're in a laboratory; things must be sterile and clean, free of pressures and desires and fears. We don't know if people can really coexist harmoniously in fulfillment, as a dynamic, without rules, without all the pressures — we don't know that it's possible. Heretofore it hasn't happened that we can see. It's fragile; sometimes the experiment is so rarefied that there's not even room for emotional or psychological stress. You can only go together to that point if everyone understands that they're engaged in a particular experiment, and there's a coordination or a cooperation taking place. If one person is imbalanced in it, then everyone else will feel the ramifications of that imbalance. When people are making vows, or saying they understand, or making commitments, then it's important that they understand the commitment they're making is not for the outer curcumstance; but the commitment is to an inner function, an inner understanding. At that point there is no separation.

S: Here there may be, as you say, a very rarefied atmosphere — people who are living very closely — whereas going out of this situation, the world is moving at different wavelengths, in conflict, in opposition.

Daniel: The world around us will mirror what's happening here. You will see your abrupt qualities; you can also see your care and comfort — you'll see it all around you.

So when people are engaged in an experiment, they've only come to that point of experimentation because they understand their need; there is a mutual understanding that change is necessary — a thorough change, not a conditioned change or change that is modification. That is the further exploration, but the basis of the exploration is that one comes to some harmony in their life, and that there is no outer circumstance that is disturbing. We're enquiring with that understanding that no harm can come to one. And in that understanding, there is a responsibility to go deeper.

So this deeper concern is also a deeper refinement — to be fixed in no way, to be on intimate terms with this energy or God, to speak to it directly and clearly; to understand how it operates, how you operate; to be on such intimate terms with this universe that you see what's appropriate and what's not appropriate; and to also be concerned that the community or those around you are also moving with the same intensity.

S: Okay, but the fact is that they aren't; and it's not clear that one can prod them.

Daniel: If you're prodding someone all the time, then you're giving them a direction; and when you're giving them a direction, you're denying them the capacity to change, to perceive. So you must see when what you call prodding is a tool of life, and when prodding becomes something violent.

The issue is not only the violence you're doing to the other, it's the violence you're doing to your own journey — you're incapacitating yourself. So it's not that anything is put aside; it's that you see what doesn't work, or you'll find out what doesn't work. We must see at one point what is theory and what is fact. If you perceive something and cannot communicate it, it's limited to theory.

So then the change that must take place must also include those around you, not just yourself and those who can hear you. Although there may be only one or two or ten who can perceive it directly, the work that you're essentially doing is not for those one or ten but with the world, the universe. So someone's angry, someone's hurt, someone's distraught and you can see why; but also, is something incorrect in how you're proceeding — can you look deeper? Yesterday you understood everything, and the memory of that prevents you from looking deeper at your situation today. So yesterday's understanding becomes today's superstructure; there is a limitation now. That's what I mean by a human being having to transcend even understanding. Yesterday I saw something so clearly that I utilize that yesterday as a basis of today. And I don't see that yesterday's perception is now a habit. So the memory of being clear yesterday becomes behavior today. I may have seen something yesterday; the challenge is to go even deeper now.

S: *So the expression of that is always going to be changing also.*

Daniel: It always must — with different people, different occasions, at different times, in different situations. And if I try to make it the same, then I become mechanical.

The challenge that came up yesterday was that when something is said and there's a feeling in that expression that's shared by others, can it be conveyed to the written word, to the page? Usually in the past, what's said and then written has lacked something — has had some quality but still lacked something. In the past the most you could hope for was that each book would be a handshake or an introduction. But now can the sense of what is happening in our lives also be conveyed to the written page, so that the reader is also undergoing a change — also recognizes the need to look deeply at life and understand it?

14 August 1978

The Essential Relationship

Daniel: Each individual is a record of everything that has ever occurred, and that record can be tapped. A question can be put in such a way as to bring forth this storehouse of information, this collection of thousands of years of human evolution. But there appears to me to be something also beyond the information and the collective history of mankind; there seems to be a universal energy there that can also be touched.

We have the impression that there's an outer world and an inner world, the impression that we are separate from what appears to be an outer universe. And inside ourselves, we are divided. But the underlying fact is that no division exists. The real basis of questioning and answering is a dialogue with oneself, is a probing of the universal; it's an inward look. The real question that matters in one's life is also the question that all of humankind is essentially asking. The real question is, who am I, what is going on, what is this life? The essential question takes great meditation.

In this discussion the interviewer has the responsibility to provide a forum — but first to recognize his own need, his own need to understand life, his own need to feel. So he therefore has the function to realize himself in the interview at the same time that he provides a forum that others can also participate in. Then the one interviewed has the responsibility to respond to that intensity. But both parties to the interview must walk away fulfilled — that is the basis for the audience to find their fulfillment. It is not entertainment, it is not a way to spend an hour or two. The listener then also has a responsibility.

S: So it seems that the basis for interaction is really the ability to share a perception — not to take on the idea of the perception, but to really share it. But then also there's the pitfall that for the continuation of that perception there is dependency upon that intensity, or that mutual experience. It appears to be a difficult area.

Daniel: That difficulty is also part of the growth, the maturity. So I'm not saying that there's no difficulty in relationship. You can find a personal realization separate from existence, separate from life around you. But the challenge will be to be able to relate, to communicate, to interact with other human beings — that's the basic challenge. Can you see that the real basis of relationship is that you're both free beings, and whatever form you use to communicate is just a form? You can have integrity in the form, but part of that integrity is to understand when to put the form aside. So the beginnings of relationship may be dependent on form. Before you can communicate to another you may have to meet; so meeting each other is dependent on form. But now, what is to be communicated is formless. This is the paradox.

In the past many so-called wise men or sages have had a heightened experience — recognized the essential oneness, the essential fact of life. Through an experience they've realized themselves, but then they've associated the realization with the experience, formulated a technique based on the experience, and taught it as a means to achieve this state. Through approaches and techniques, you may come to the threshhold of experience. But the actual discovery of love or God cannot be brought about through any technique. All techniques, all forms, all approaches are coming out of thought. Essentially there is no approach to what you are. You are — you don't have to approach it.

S: So all that you're really doing, then, in talking, is exhausting that area of form; but really it's not possible to go into the formless through another.

Daniel: There is no 'other' — the only reason that it's *not* possible to do it with another is because you don't realize that there is no 'other'. We have this structure that you must do it yourself, you must see it yourself, you must be your own guru. We've created this structure of separation when actually we're interdependent. When I feel I must have my own experience, I must be free, what does that freedom mean? Does it mean the absence of fondness, the absence of relationship? That's absurd. I understand that there is no separation, and when there is no separation there's nothing to be free *from*. I'm a prisoner of my thoughts, of my ideas, my reactions, my fears and my conditions. The real relationship is beyond words.

S: *What is necessary to go into the formless?*

Daniel: The basis of formlessness is purity in yourself, refinement in yourself. When you understand that the outer structure is not the thing alone, then you look at yourself — every movement, every nuance, every attempt. In that looking a purification takes place. At this point integrity is necessary — to understand your need, to formulate your need, to see what you're after and understand what you're doing.

S: *We can see the form, but we also see that the form isn't working; so it doesn't seem that we can see what we're after, but only what isn't working.*

Daniel: Because we're looking for something that form cannot satisfy, that's all. I look at a mate or a hoped-for mate, and I'm attracted by her physical beauty or an impression she makes on me. I'm attracted to the person as an object, yet I'm looking for love; can I understand that I won't find love in the object? When you've turned a person into an object, then it's convenience. And a marriage of convenience will collapse.

S: *As the mind moves into a relatively quiet state, it's very difficult at that point to see what the reality is — whether it's just a more expansive projection, a total sedation, or whether it's real.*

Daniel: Then wait until it's clear. Because reality is not hidden. If you're unclear whether what you're doing is a conditioned movement or a full response, then wait until there's no doubt about it. That capacity to wait when necessary is full action — the capacity to realize that you're confused, that you don't know what to do. Waiting is the relationship, waiting is the dynamic, waiting is the fulfillment. Out of the waiting, no violence takes place; and in that waiting, in that stillness, love can enter. Waiting is the ending of the continuity of thought. When a thought comes and you pursue it, this is continuity; the body is activated through the thought process — it doesn't question it. So the first step is the realization that you don't know — you don't know if this is lust or love — but you care enough to find out. I need to understand it, I need to feel it. And I know now that I don't feel it fully.

So I've discovered that I don't know how to proceed, and that discovery is the basis of waiting. In that waiting there's a dynamic — let me see, let me investigate more, let me be silent, let me examine. Because it's important enough to me that I understand. Life is precious to me now. When life is precious, you will not repeat the blunders of the past, the abuse of the past, the entanglements of the past. Because now you have something essential to do. And then waiting is also essential. That waiting is the soil for the seed of love to grow.

S: But it also seems that the opposite of waiting is restlessness.

Daniel: Full, dynamic waiting has no opposite. I'm talking about a waiting that understands that it's choiceless in its waiting. When you don't know what to do, and life is precious, then you don't want to waste another hour, another minute, another year. It's a dynamic state, and you're not in the marketplace for artificiality.

S: But to me, the waiting that I seem to experience is a waiting for a state.

Daniel: Waiting is not for anything — waiting is a dynamic quality. Mind only has a past or a future, it only has a this or a that.

When it hears the word waiting it goes into opposites — you're either waiting for something in the future or you're killing time. I don't know what to do, I have competing thoughts, I have so much pressure, and in that I find that I'm helpless. So I'm not waiting for anything, I'm not helpless in order to obtain something. The fact is that I don't know what to do. Yet I'm eager, I'm curious, I'm vital — I need to live, I need to understand. The basic understanding is that I don't know — but can I wait? That is the clarity, that is what I mean in saying that waiting is the soil. That waiting is a complete action, and the answer comes in that waiting. Waiting is the dynamic that allows you to respond to the answer, to merge with the answer.

So waiting is the break with the continuity of thought, waiting is the break of the link from past to future — waiting is the basis of the present. Then we go deeper into this state of waiting. Waiting is the understanding that great care is necessary in life, attention is necessary in life, refinement is necessary in life.

S: But how does that dynamic quality manifest? I'm not able to totally understand how that dynamic quality can exist within that understanding of not-knowing.

Daniel: Until this point, we're operating through the intellect; and the intellect is just a storehouse of memory and conditionings that have come out of memory. It is a continuity from past to future. Up until this point we're operating solely from intellect — it instructs us how to behave, how to move, how to relate. Yet the evidence that's piling up around us is that each one of our relationships, each one of our contacts and movements turns out to be limited. The evidence around us indicates that the instrument that we're using is not a full instrument; it's incomplete. So as I look around me, I see that the information I've acquired or accumulated is not the sole answer.

The realization that you don't know is the last thought. That 'not-knowing' is thought's understanding of its limitations. Now many approaches in the past have attempted to bring you to this state by baffling the thought process, by throwing the mind back on itself, or short-circuiting it in one way or another. My feeling is that through many of these techniques you also damage something, you correspondingly destroy something. You create further images, and the basic premise is that thought is a villain. So I don't feel that thought is a villain that has to be stopped. My feeling is that the thinker must understand its limitations. And waiting is the manifestation of this understanding.

You see, the thinker thinks that it knows — it thinks it knows everything. The discovery by the thinker that it doesn't know the essential expresses itself as "I don't know". When the knower discovers that it doesn't know and cannot know, whatever it does, it has come to the end of thought, to the end of itself — not by trying to shut itself up, but because as a response to life it has seen its limitations; it doesn't know. It doesn't know what God is, what feeling is, what love is, what marriage is, what male and female are. It doesn't know these things and it realizes it. It realizes that everything that it's been taught about life does not equal life. It realizes that all its books and all its information on 'how to' doesn't allow it to bridge the gap. And this may happen to the individual in a single incident. When the moment is right and the being needs to understand, then the basis of understanding is there. The incident will manifest, the incident will take place — a word, a phrase, a face, a morning rain; a teacher, a guru, a look, anything. I would say that the incident has taken place for most of us, and not in some mysterious way. That fulfillment is available if you recognize your need, if you approach it with care. The secrets of the universe lie within you, and they're at hand.

S: But there's nothing volitionally that we can do at this point other than just simply pay attention — there's nothing to do to bring about this surrender or this 'don't know' state except to look at what we are.

Daniel: First feel it so strongly, so deeply — first taste it — and then volition has a place. But it's not an act of volition on your part or my part, it's an expression that comes out of intelligence. It's

The Essential Relationship   95

not that "I want to do this", but that one sees what is necessary, sees the need.

S: So if one's feeling is only to sit, one would just go meditate, and that's all?

Daniel: Don't let this idea of meditation be an escape. To my mind, meditation is a full response. To sit down to meditate means by its very nature that you're in touch with something. And this sitting is a further invitation to this energy to enter and express itself. So having touched this softness, having been touched by it, then sitting may be the movement necessary to absorb it more fully, to invite it more fully. It must be a vital state, not something that you're using as a tranquillizer. If you're using it as a tranquillizer, then please understand that's what you're doing, and don't call it anything more than that.

S: Sitting has always seemed to me the most direct way to cut through; that seems to have been the impetus in the past. But now I'm wondering if the cutting through is in itself the problem.

Daniel: Yes, because when you're cutting through, you may be cutting through something essential. So my feeling is that you don't have to cut through these things as much as that they fall away when you understand their nature.

S: Then sitting is only an expression of nothing else happening.

Daniel: Meditation is a real interest in what's going on around you — and if thought happens to be going on, I don't see why you can't meditate on the thought process, to see what it's saying, see what it wants — it's expressing something. You're understanding that thought is expressing itself, it's saying something. Your attempt to get rid of it only gives it a greater impetus to continue. So it's not really a question of cutting through, it's a question of hearing, seeing what it's saying, understanding it if it's possible — then it may fall away. My feeling is that meditation is a real interest in life, it's a real zest for life, it's a vital quality of interest in what's going on inside and around one. It doesn't have any idea beforehand. You're really investigating, really finding out.

So once one understands the need to wait as a vital response, that waiting takes you deeper. In that moment you see where volition is necessary and where it is not. But it is no longer a volition that comes out of the thought process of the thinker, that says "I want this, this is nice for me"; it has no 'me' attached to it. Volition is now a response to a challenge; it sees the need, and it sees the individual need and the collective need as being one and the same. Then volition is charged — not with the entity but charged with the universal need. So if you come to peace in your life then you may also, through volition, be able to manifest this peace on earth. After realization, after understanding, you may use the techniques and the formulas as a means of communication. But this is not self-aggrandizement, it is not pushing your own program; you're seeing the need and you're responding. And when you see that the tools you're using no longer apply, you're able to put them aside. You're not defining yourself by an approach.

As I am introduced to a world of form and formlessness, then I can understand freedom — when I can't hurt anything, when life is precious. The need is to go beyond the form, and have such an underlying affection that violence can't take place. Only in that being touched and touching, only when one feels that universal energy or God in oneself, only then can one go beyond the form. Then there's no higher and lower. When you realize that, then you are seeing with compassion. You and what you see are one — you see the need for form and you also see the need for formlessness, and you're moving in and out with no problem, no prison. Then life is not a mystery, because it's not separate from you. When you have that curiosity and that zest to discover and find out, then you're viewing whatever's going on around you with a passion, with a need to understand.

S: It seems that everything that needs to have been heard has been heard at this point.

Daniel: When we've come to a situation of no more questions — actually come to that point — then we're living in a world of perception. Every pore, every cell is affected by that. At one point a merger takes place in which there's no separation between beings; they understand their underlying need, they understand what they are to each other, and they understand there's no separation.

S: And dependence isn't a problem any more.

Daniel: Dependence doesn't exist. Freedom and life won't allow it to exist. When you understand that life is relationship, and that you are life, and it's all interdependent, there are no such things as opposites any longer. So all that's in that relationship is this sense of wonder — or looking deeper, of finding out more about the universe and yourself. It's an understanding of the need to look deeper and deeper.

And the further challenge is that it's expressed outwardly, that it's communicated. When life and you are one movement, then you see that the challenge of communication is always yours. In the past, you may have touched some greatness in interaction with another — something took place in you and you associated it with the other — and then you didn't want to let the other go. But there must be a natural coming and going, a physical coming and going if you are to be free, if you're to find a full expression, if you're to feel. It can't be clinging, because clinging doesn't allow freedom to manifest, love to manifest or relationship to manifest. Clinging is the denial of your very being and of life around you. The essential relationship, the essential love is that you are freely moving together and there is no real separation — whether of five feet, ten feet, or ten thousand miles. The interrelationships of the universe and of life around us is in each relationship that we're having now. There's no longer a separation.

My feeling is that the relationship cannot merge fully, the perception cannot take place, until that fundamental fact is understood — that what you experience is what you are. The relationship between beings and inside yourself is the relationship to the universe. You must probe that, you must discover the dimensions of that relationship, so that the relationship has a dynamic quality always. It must mature and grow.

That freedom is the basis of real relationship — not clinging or self-definition. We must take this relationship out into the world, out into the community, and express it. Find out. Find its limitations, see the vastness, experience it. Because the essential relationship is a full understanding inside yourself; it must filter down to every cell in your body. It must be your experience. So that's the difference between perception and instruction. At this point instruction is not your experience, perception is your experience — you see it and you live by it.

Can we feel first? Can we wait? Can we see the importance of waiting and reflecting, taking that moment? Then sitting has a dynamic quality, it has an afterglow, a feeling to it; it's not forcing yourself to do this or do that, to put in your required time. And when you see that you have this need and feeling to sit, and go through life in a reflective manner, to watch and understand, your social situation will allow you to do that. The reason that many of us have a social situation that doesn't allow us to do that is because we've never really thought it was important enough. If we really think it's important enough, life provides. In our jobs, in our schools, in our homes we haven't provided for it; we have never personally thought that it was important enough, and so therefore our society has never made room for it. When it's important, there's room for it; life provides the time — more than enough time. If the individual needs to understand life, if he has that dynamic quality, he's provided for. There's a blessing in that. To understand that blessing, to understand that loveliness is essential if you're going to continue, if you're going to go deeper.

So to understand that the job you have or the home you have or the parents you have is a direct expression of what you are at this given moment, is to understand your challenge. There is no further movement until you come to peace with what you've created, until you understand its operations and its workings. So if this meditation you've experienced in the past was an attempt to escape from the world around you, it was not meditation at all, it was not waiting at all. Waiting is not an attempt to make the outer go away. Waiting takes place when your outer world is put in such order that you're receptive for God to come into your heart — just now.

20 August 1978

The Language of Silence

Joseph: I see that there's a strong movement to hold onto something to do for tomorrow, so that I'll be needed. I see that whole mechanism operating, and yet it goes on.

Daniel: But you invent a tomorrow for yourself today. Understand the price for that. In that continuity, one is not living fully. You are insuring your continuity. Mind is constantly projecting into the future in order to insure its survival, and the price of this psychological survival is the absence of real love, is the absence of any meaning. This projection equals mediocrity. Whatever you achieve through that continuity has no substance. Thought cannot provide the sort of security necessary. There is only one energy that can provide that security; and only if you touch that essence will you be assured. Without touching that, you can accumulate and accumulate, and you'll still live in lack.

And you cannot experience that quality artificially — through breathing methods, through any technical approach. There is no approach to what you are. But in order to touch that essence you may need to go through the superficial layers, the conditioned layers; and any time that you are going through those layers you will know great pressure. All of history — your own personal history, and the collective history of mankind, is recorded in you. So any attempt even to see reality beyond yourself, beyond your own conditioning, may be met by great pressure. It is not something to undertake off-handedly, because the very insight demands a further look; and the further look means that you're introduced to a vastness — you've gone beyond the personal into the collective. And then you understand that the collective is also limited.

The Language of Silence

So it is a journey without end. That journey without end requires great psychological preparation. There's no returning, there's no 'back'. Right now, collectively, we've limited ourselves to the world of psychology and explanation without substance — this equals that, that equals this. This is again the problem-solving mentality. Psychology will be the next problem that man is creating. It's an attempt to define, to name; and through that definition, to use. We've limited ourselves in the last century to therapy, not to essence. And most of the approaches developed in the last few years are exactly that — therapy. But if you never understand the essence, and you're constantly treating the wound, you may through your therapy actually be reinforcing the wound, reinforcing the illness. It's my view that we've come to a point in life where now, in treating the illusion, we're actually supporting it, reinforcing it.

Dan: You say that psychological preparation is necessary. Can you expand on that?

Daniel: The psychological preparation is to ascertain — directly, clearly and precisely — what you need. Because along the way, there may be great distractions and pressures. You've accumulated so much in your life, and you've created so many expectations in others in your life. You have created a framework around yourself, a satellite system around yourself; and this structure now requires you to maintain it, to continue a form of behavior. Any change in that behavior will also rattle the structure you've built around you.

This point is very important. You may be married, and have children; and the basis of your marriage may have been loneliness or fear, or the desire to have a companion, or something to reinforce yourself; and through that you may have created a family structure, and then a community around you. So it's a mutual support system. Now you may come to an understanding that the support system may also be your limitation, your prison. So it's not just a question of overthrowing the support system, it's a question of coming to a deep understanding in your life that essentially you don't need the support system — you see that there's nothing to support. Reality doesn't need to be supported. Essence needs no support. What has needed support in my life is something that's false; that falseness constantly needs feedback or reassurance. The very reassurance that I seek may indicate the non-substance in my position.

When I understand that I don't need support, there's an inner change that has happened. That inner change, that softness, that aloneness — aloneness simply meaning that you are no longer demanding support and reassurance, because you've touched something of quality in yourself — that aloneness as a dynamic looks at the world. That aloneness has experienced a personal freedom. Now, aloneness needs to find a means of communication. Because the fuller freedom takes place in relationship.

Aloneness is then the basis for communication and relationship. Aloneness is the basis for the communication of essence — essence to essence.

D: *What do you mean by communication?*

Daniel: To communicate a quality of love.

D: *By being it?*

Daniel: By being it. But now, when you see further, you see that there's a collective sorrow. You've touched something, but humanity is going in this cycle of events over and over and over again; they're creating pain and sorrow, momentary pleasure, war and misery; but essentially not touching something deeply. You may have personally touched it, but it's not your personal possession. In experiencing it, in immersing yourself in that energy, in touching the source, the next challenge is to find a means of communication. Because there's a further refinement necessary — not that the essence needs refinement; but that the expression needs to perfect itself.

When a person has actually touched this essential quality, then the situation in which he finds himself in the society is an indication of his need to go deeper personally. If there is anger or fear or hurt in response to what you've said, that anger or fear or hurt is now a guideline for you. The lack of communication is yours, because you are the one who has touched the need to communicate. You understand that personal freedom by itself has no meaning; that freedom only has meaning in relationship. Having come to a relative health yourself personally, having come to a freedom yourself personally, you now understand that the world's pain is your pain; if the world is in pain, if there's a collective sorrow, you're not free from it. So that's your further freedom, that's your further refinement — not that you feel personal pain or personal sorrow, but that you see the collective sorrow that exists. And in touching this essential quality in yourself, through the collective sorrow you experience compassion, a quality of deep feeling — not *for* anything or anyone, just deep feeling. You see, compassion, or feeling, or this essence, has no name — has no condition, has no power; it just is pure, and it belongs to no one. In touching it, a change has happened in you. In experiencing it deeply and looking outward, a change is also taking place around you. You can't measure it. If you need excellence in yourself, if you understand the need, if the thirst for essence is great in you, then you'll start to understand that a change is happening around you also. So it is only in touching depth in yourself that in effect a change is taking place, a change that you could never manage or direct — because it is not coming from you.

D: *Do you even recognize it while it's happening?*

Daniel: You must. Recognition seems to me to be very important now, because without that recognition, irresponsibility takes place. Any time that the merger is not complete, thought will enter; and thought will then organize; and the only reason that thought organizes is for its own perpetuation, its own self-perpetuation. So this recognition is a consciousness of what is happening — not as a center, but just a pure consciousness of what is taking place, and your responsibility to it.

You see, what is happening now is that once you've touched

this quality, thought, as the thinker, must be responsible to it. In the past, thought was never responsible to its expression. Now, when thought is the servant of essence, thought is responsibility. It doesn't over-promise, it doesn't over-project. Its promise, its expression, its words, are in line with the need. So we come to a point where essence and form are working together, are one movement; we come to a point where having experienced that essential quality in life, thought is now in the service of that quality. So what we have at that point is a whole human being, a total movement. That total movement must have an effect. It's in harmony with the universe.

At this point, your life is not your own, at this point your life is not your personal property or your personal possession. At this point of deep enquiry, you've touched some universal quality. Once you've touched this universal quality, it speaks — and it speaks precisely and clearly.

D: *What's its language?*

Daniel: Its language is silence. When you've touched silence, that silence will speak through you in a language that others will understand — the only true language is silence.

2 July 1979

A Deepening Yearning

Daniel: We discover that in the past, we have only known desire *for,* longing *for* something, to achieve something; and achievement is usually related to matter — something out there, through time and space, that will enhance me; or something out there, that once I achieve it, will give life more meaning and more depth. Throughout most of our lives, in that achievement, we find that what we achieve is still lacking, still limited; it doesn't provide, it doesn't fill up that emptiness. In fact, it seems to be only in the pursuit of a goal that life *had* any meaning. Once we achieve a goal, it seems that we revert back to this dissatisfied state.

In totally seeing that the pursuit of the object in the future is a waste of energy, that it is not the way — thoroughly not the way — one experiences a deep feeling of not knowing what to do; because one's whole life was always engaged in doing, pursuing, activity. Now there's no avenue open to me any longer. If I don't know what to do, if the projected goal is seen to be limited, without any redeeming feature, I'm no longer able to pursue it. In that simple discovery of not knowing what to do, my activity ceases, my outer pursuit ceases; I'm alone in that. When I am alone in that, a great yearning awakens. I still need, but I cannot acquire anymore. I realize that whatever I acquire is still limited, whatever I do is limited.

In the silence that ensues with that understanding, I experience yearning. When I experience yearning, it deepens. And when I experience the deepening quality of this yearning, I am now involved in a journey within.

When we meet here now, having collectively experienced this

quality of stillness, and the yearning, this need to understand, this need to live fully — we meet in a deep affection. In that affection, can the question be your responsibility, can it be a mutual responsibility — that before we leave this room, something will be clearly understood and seen? It is our need to understand, it is our need to experience, our need to live fully, and all the information that we have acquired, what we think we are before we come into the room, doesn't serve, doesn't help. So can the question come from that quality of yearning, can it come from silence?

Joseph: To me this yearning quality seems to come out of pain, and when I become exhausted in going outward to find a solution, some energy comes in and there's a clarity. When that pain comes to rest, it seems like something steps in and stops the going deeper — and this contact with this quality of yearning seems to end.

Daniel: You say that you experience it sometimes, and then it seems to pass away. Something takes place, and the experience of divinity, the experience of fulfillment, the experience of love and relationship seems to just collapse, be destroyed.

J: So what has happened?

Daniel: So then the question is, "Is life, or is this energy something that comes and goes?" Because all I have experienced in my life is something that comes and goes. Why does it come and go? Where does it go? Where does it come from? So obviously, the experience has not been a thorough one.

Dan: Nor the failure.

Daniel: In this movement now, there's no failure; there's only absence. Absence indicates that a change has happened; absence does not indicate failure. Absence indicates that there's a need in you. You touch something, you experience it — you are not separate from it. And the next moment some incident occurs, something happens, and this immensity that you've experienced a moment before seems to vanish. But when you experience immensity, there is no vanishing point; it doesn't have that kind of definition. It's not enclosed, it's not something that can be put aside or collected. So where does it go? When I look at it, I see that there is no 'go'. It hasn't gone anywhere. But the attention, the oneness is now somewhere else in me. I am distracted; something else calls me. The refinement is not deep enough.

So the yearning by itself is the introduction, is the first step, is the essential stepping-stone. Now the need is to see if there is something that is full and total — that doesn't lessen. Is there something that is eternal? And then at that point I recognize: how can I contain something eternal and immense if I am also not that quality myself? So the challenge is now in front of me. I see that what I call up and down, or coming and going, is actually my inability to experience totally. When I recognize the need for a total experience, I am now setting the stage for one.

At that point I have no other life. Life to me is that breath, life to me is that essence, and I therefore need to experience that essence in all things — in everything I do, all the time. A part-time essence or a part-time immensity now to me is limited, is an in-between state. So now I ask the question, where does it go? I ask it directly — I can't live without it. When I ask that question, I receive an answer; because that question that comes from deep yearning is a question of the heart, a question that is unabashed, unafraid — a question that has a need. Once that question is asked with such an intensity, the answer, the response must be forthcoming; it must be of the same quality as the question.

So this energy appears to go, because I have not invited it deeper in my life, into my heart. But now I experience it, and when I experience the absence, I experience a great need, a great yearning to even go deeper than that, and I invite it — it must be with me at all times, I must be it. Because when I experience this immensity, what I am experiencing is a deep change inside myself; even physically, a change is taking place. My capacity is also expanding; with this experience my capacity to go deeper is also expanding, is also changing.

You can only see what you are prepared to see. And when the

need is great, the preparation is also great — you prepare to see everything, to look at everything. There is no independent investment in anything being any way.

D: *You just said that when you ask that question with that need, there is an answer that is from the heart. How do we recognize that the answer is true? Is there a quality to that language that's recognizable, that's distinct, that's clear?*

Daniel: You see, the answer should never require your belief. The answer should never require that you be hypnotized, or that you avoid, or anything like that. So when the question is an actual question coming from deep within, when there's a need to understand deeply, then the response will leave no residue. It's not that it's clear in this moment; it's clear eternally.

D: *It doesn't need a paragraph to back it up.*

Daniel: It doesn't need any reinforcement or any reassurance. So when you have come to a point in your life where you're asking an essential question — where the need is really strong in you and it's recognized — you cannot live with or accept an artificial response. But when you are only moving from the intellectual plane, then what you are seeking is reinforcement, or some therapeutic answer to allow you to get through the next hour or the next evening — some form of stimulation. An actual answer to a question of the heart has no stimulation. There is nothing to debate, there is nothing to believe in, there is nothing to doubt. So this will be the only way for one to understand, to know what is true.

I cannot believe or trust in the truth outwardly, and I cannot trust myself to be truthful; I see that I'm fragmented, and I see that the outer world is fragmented also. The yearning for truth is there, and I see that I can't depend on myself or the outer to supply it. Find out if there is anything true in you, anything clear or definite in you. And when or if you touch a point inside yourself where you say, yes, this is true — I see it clearly, it is not *my* truth, it is truth; it has substance, it has quality — and when you touch that inside yourself, then ask the question. And if the response is equal to the question, and without residue — then you have just invited relationship into your life.

So what I am saying is that realization is your basis for living. It's not that you will become enlightened through some activity, through time and space — but that if you are to live in this society, if you are to live in relationship, enlightenment is a must — now. It has immediacy for you. And when it has immediacy for you, you will find that the response will be forthcoming — it can't fail. God is a response to your yearning. Love is a response to your capacity to love.

So what has happened to you in life is an exact response to the condition you're in. If you are no longer complaining, no longer pointing a finger, then you understand that what you have experienced in life, what you see outwardly, is what you are. If you need something beyond that, you must be beyond that yourself. If you need to experience truth, then you must be truth yourself.

D: *There seems to be a difference in the way you're using the term yearning to the way I have known it. Some time ago in my life things happened so that I wanted to go beyond — or whatever the phrase. And I would identify with the most recent book, or personality, and each time it didn't work; and there was still a yearning for more. But it seems that the yearning you are talking about isn't that yearning for, even though it is identified with the same general idea, like self-realization.*

Daniel: So yearning *for* is the only thing you know. We're taught a value system, we're taught a point of view at an early age, and so for us, as far as we know, yearning is a way of accumulating; and through the accumulating, we become. The amount of your accumulation will indicate to you your worth.

D: *Is this what you would call spiritual materialism?*

Daniel: This materialism is very important; it is important also that it's not artificially interrupted. Because then what will take place is that you'll transfer this accumulation to a different form — you will try what is called spirituality, or some different accumulation, or a different approach to accumulation. And then if you also adopt one of these Eastern approaches, which say that detachment or non-attachment or non-accumulation are necessary, then you're accumulating points — you are becoming something through the non-accumulation. So you see, mind is a very clever instrument; it's finding a way to continue. And it continues through reinforcement and feedback.

Now when I look at it, I understand that God or love is not feedback, it is devoid of feedback; it's not personal in nature. It's pure. There's no reward in it, there's no punishment in it. The world of reward and punishment and feedback is created by mankind. But the universe has nothing to do with that thought construct.

So, what is yearning? I see that there is no object in this life that will satisfy. There's nothing now that I can attain that will satisfy. What I need cannot be satisfied by something man-made, by something artificial, by some projection of thought. So the yearning, the need is still there, but the ability to satisfy it intellectually is no longer there. I see the limitation in anything that I can buy, sell, dream up or project. When I see the folly of pursuit, I come to rest. The need is still great, but the outer activity ceases. So now, to me yearning is life itself. And when it's absent, I know it. I can't live life any longer as a sometimes state. I must investigate, enquire — my whole life now is in the service of that quality.

3 July 1979

The Response to a Human Being

Joseph: You were saying earlier that when the yearning disappears, then I may be able, with real intensity, with a real question, to ask where this yearning has gone — where did it go? It seems to me that this is a big if; that really has to be what is happening, to be your real intensity. It seems like without a thorough defeat of all pursuits, you can't really ask that question.

Daniel: We've come to a point in our lives where through age, or accumulation, or whatever, we see we can't be satisfied with what we have. And we also see that a personalized existence doesn't provide, essentially. And we have also seen the failure of communism, totalitarianism, democracy, Marxism — we see it's an attempt at something greater than that, but we also understand the inherent failure in it. It's still governed by thought, still limited by thought.

So now we have all come to this point where life is not a personal experience, and it's also not a collective experience. And we don't want to sit here in a room and just go into a hypnotic trance. We see that nothing will be served by that. And when you actually can perceive that nothing can be served by something, you are not pressured by it any longer. So we are in a situation now where life is not personal, there is nothing to achieve or acquire in it; and we also collectively understand that hypnosis is not the way, a new party system is not the way, group therapy is not the way. So now, we have experienced and are experiencing something beyond that. But now it can no longer be called something beyond that. We must experience it so thoroughly that it's not a sometimes thing.

Because only in immersing yourself in the yearning, only in immersing yourself in a full feeling, will you be able to communicate it. And communicating it is the obvious next step in feeling.

You've come to a point in your life where you're free personally, where you're no longer governed by thought, where you're no longer pressured; you're no longer pursuing, no longer marching or shouting slogans; you're essentially free to experience and feel, thoroughly and deeply. But now the rest of humankind is not free. The rest of humankind is in hurt. So now you see that there's a collective bondage, there is a collective hurt, there is a collective sorrow. You yourself may not be experiencing the personal sorrow or the collective sorrow, but when you look around you, you see that it is taking place. And you also see your helplessness in it, that actively there is nothing you can do to help. That collective sorrow forces you to go deeper into yourself, because you recognize that the body of humankind is also you — you see your connection to all life.

So when you no longer have the outer activity, then the journey is inward. And as you have a deeper experience of this immensity, there's an outer effect. Now the challenge is to find a means of communication — not a communication that comes from the thought process, not a communication that comes from the center called 'me'; but a communication that comes from that immensity, a communication that comes from that silence. That is your challenge. Because freedom only has meaning in relationship. Your freedom means nothing if your family is in hunger and pain, if your community is being destroyed.

So you have only experienced personal freedom so that you can introduce freedom to your life and to the life around you. But it is not a mission. You're not a self-elected official. The pain around you is forcing you to experience deeper; and the deeper experience is also finding a means of communication. You're not communicating from self to self, you're communicating from essence to essence. If you feel that quality deeply in yourself, you will be able to perceive that quality in another. When you see that quality, that potential in the other, something is taking place — a connection is made. You'll find the language, you'll find a way.

And as you find a way, you're also going deeper in yourself, because you'll be challenged. All the pressures, all the violence in the society will challenge you, will throw you back on yourself, will force you, again and again and again, to touch that source.

So there's a refining process that is taking place. It is no longer failure, it is no longer guilt or anything like that. In every situation you discover your limitation; and each time you discover your limitation, your helplessness, you go deeper, you find a way.

Dan: All of this comes out of this silence, out of that immense energy. What is the difference in degree — because it all seems to be the same essential energy, it all seems to be in that deep silence.

Daniel: So then God is a response to a human being. When the need is great, when this yearning is great and is experienced as great, when it is experienced as a total movement, then what you are seeing is what you are. At that point there are no words. So there may be a distinction intellectually, between God and compassion and love and energy; but at that point, when you are not separate from it all, then you understand that God is not the word, energy is not the word, love is not the word; the word is just a symbol. But inherent in the symbol is silence. If you can hear the silence in the word, then you also are silence. What can see silence, what can experience silence except silence itself? What can experience love except love itself? What can experience God except God? What can experience compassion except compassion? So you must be what you experience — you're not separate from it. There is no space, there is no definition at that point. And that is the only way to understand what is true — to be truth yourself, to live it. Because you must live what you see; you can't compromise your heart at that point.

So I am talking about a thorough transformation, a thorough realization, a thorough enlightenment — not one that comes and goes, not one that takes a position. And I'm talking about the enlightenment of a normal, average person, in his own society. Because that's where the challenge is great — not in some figurehead who sits above, or removed from it all, but in our everyday activity in life. Once you understand that it is available, that it is possible, can you live without it? If you had no inkling that love existed or that life was full, then you could just live according to any plan or program. But once you know, deeply, that there is a quality of life that you are not living in totally, or experiencing fully, you need it.

D: *In the past I have experienced this need — in time. Does the yearning cut through time?*

Daniel: Yearning cuts through everything. Because without it being a full yearning, what takes place is a psychological construct; it's a way to achieve a certain state.

D: *So then the time is the refining process?*

Daniel: We have created time; we put off things through time. When we have created psychological time, we have found a way to survive intellectually through tomorrow, six months from now, a year from now.

So there may be moments when we have an experience, but then thought again re-enters and is able to capitalize on the experience, to make it personal. So what takes place in our problem-making and problem-solving is that we never actually solve the problem. And that is why there's a continuity of problem-making and problem-solving. So the solution to the problem is not only to resolve the issue at hand, the solution to the problem is to understand this entity that is constantly constructing problems, and why it does it.

So yearning is the quality that cuts through the framework, that cuts through the excess. When you really yearn for love, romance is meaningless to you. When you're really hungry, junk food has no meaning. When you are eager for reality, you won't settle for anything less. If you need the experience, you will not settle for an intellectual construct, for an explanation. We've only accepted the false in the past because we ourselves are false. What we have accepted in the past is something to soothe us or to reinforce our framework, our entity. And the need is to love: we yearn for love. And it is not a dumb state, it's an intelligent state — it is something that can be proven, demonstrated, perceived, felt, touched, tasted, and explained. If it cannot be, there's a question about it.

3 July 1979

The Qualities of Resistance

Daniel: Is there anything that is dependable and reliable, eternal, not limited by thought, time or space? Everything, upon examination, seems to have an essential failing. It ages, it decays, it dies. So we now collectively come to this point, where there's no meaning that we can think of, and yet there is a yearning in our life to experience something real, something of essence. What happens to you when you see that? When you see that your own thought process and your conditioning is unreliable, and you see that the promises that are made around you are also unreliable, and you can't trust in this form any longer? And yet the need is great, the passion is great, the yearning to touch the real is there. At that point there is a sharpness — a sharpness which is not cleverness, which is not sophisticated, which is not cynical — a sharpness where the whole being, the whole body, everything, is attuned; everything is sharp, waiting, looking, examining, yearning. The whole of life is there in front of you. That is the moment of relationship, that is the moment of real enquiry.

Joseph: I come right to the point of perception or feeling or passion, and then all of a sudden there's a direct movement out of it.

Daniel: What is taking place in that? Let's understand that. Because from what we can see, who is resisting it? What is the quality of the resistance? By what means does it resist? See when it comes up in you. Because there are ten thousand years of recorded history there — and history works through con-

The Qualities of Resistance 117

tinuity. And now I'm coming to a point where there's no longer a continuity, there's a freshness. And the freshness is devoid of 'me', is the ending of 'me' — not the collapse of me, or the destruction of me; but I see at that point that there is a vastness that I know nothing of. And I am eager to experience that, to immerse myself in that, to learn from it, to feel it. And at a certain moment there's a resistance to it, there's a movement completely away from it. So now what is happening, is that this point — when I see what I would call resistance — is a signal to me that the yearning isn't great enough, that the passion is not strong enough.

J: Why not?

Daniel: Because I don't understand the issue, I don't understand what is at hand. So instead of fighting with this thing I call resistance, instead of struggling with it, can I see that it is history — it is the tradition, it is the continuity of thought over thousands of years, it is the collective experience. I may have calmed my private existence, but now I am also plugged into a collective that has great force and great power; and it can exert great pressure. Because when I am moving to an experience through passion, I stand alone. I am the human race, I am alone, and in that experience something is taking place in the universe around me; it is having an effect. But it is also testing me. The tradition, the very cellular structure is also resisting, pulling back. At the same time that I'm yearning, at the same time that there's a passion, there's also a resistance — recorded history, all of human history is resisting that change.

It's not to fight with it. It's to understand that there is a need for a greater preparation. So when this so-called resistance takes place, that is the signal to go even deeper. That signal is an important signal. Because at that moment, you can only look when you're free to do so. At that moment, what is the nature of this thing you call resistance? Can you, with that same passion of a moment ago, now look at this so-called resistance? Can you, with that same passion, understand it? Can you

118   *in that stillness . . .*

understand that human call, can you understand the historical call? Can you understand the entanglements?

At the same time that there is a collective need, a universal need to merge, to understand, there has also been a time-bound resistance to that understanding. You can experience it individually, and you can also see its nature collectively. You can see that throughout the centuries there has been a yearning for something beyond the form, and at the same time a great clinging to the form. You can see that collectively there has been a yearning for love, a love beyond 'me', with no definition, no dimension — beyond the construct. And at the same time there is a habit of constructing everything, or organizing everything, or attaching myself to everything as my personal property. Collectively and individually, we've declared things our personal property; and yet at the same time that there is this great pressure to own everything, we want some beauty that is free, not owned by anyone. I see it. And the habit is strong. And I understand that the habit comes out of a deep insecurity, out of a deep sense of loss. When that sense of loss is there, I try to get the beauty of the world to enhance me, I cling to it, I hold on to it; I possess it in the hopes that its light will reflect on me.

But now I understand the need to touch that light so thoroughly that what is called 'me' and light no longer exist in separation. To experience that light, to experience that essence, is the ending of the resistance called 'me', the ending of the separation, the ending of the duality. And I see as I approach it, that there is still resistance somewhere, a subtle conditioning somewhere; that's my signal to go deeper. So I have put aside the personal conditioning, and now I have experienced the collective conditioning. And when I understand the nature of this collective conditioning, I now experience a subtle conditioning, millions of years old. And when I have experienced that thoroughly, and I go even deeper than that, I experience the very conditioning inherent in form. Form itself is inherently conditioned; for form to be form, it needs a pattern of energy. So I am going deeper through that signal. And I'm going deeper through the signal, not as an act of volition, but only because the need is great; the need to understand everything along the way is great — to push nothing aside, to fight with nothing, to struggle with nothing. I need to be free. And freedom is the capacity to look, to understand, to avoid nothing.

In this moment, we have gone through a personal history, the collective history, and the history inherent in form. Now where are we? We come to a point in our exploration that there is no reference point, there's nothing to refer to. And you also come to a point where you don't need to refer to anything. You are touching a sea of energy and essence; and through that essence, look. In touching that quality in life, in touching the source, now look; now move through the society, now do whatever you have to do — now go to work, now eat your meals, now have your family, now get married if you see it is fit. Now meditate — but only when you are meditation itself, only when you are the experience itself, only when you are the source itself; not as an idea, because again you understand that the idea will be inherently violent. Because this energy cannot be utilized by you personally. It has no name, it is not owned by anyone. In fact, when you touch it and experience it, there is no 'you' there. When this energy expresses itself through your form, there is no personal motive. That energy is compassion, and what will be expressed through that energy will also be compassionate.

The purpose of these last few talks was to experience what we are essentially. And it would be my larger feeling that we must find a way to convey the quiet in the room, the stillness in the room through the written page, so that others who have a similar yearning will be able to share with us in the experience.

4 July 1979

Coming to the Point of Stillness

Michael: *I seem to use a weeding-out process of negation, instead of looking for positive things to conclude. What must be is relationship without an image or past information — but the impasse, if there is any impasse at all, seems to be that I can't come here empty. If I could, there would be no need to come.*

Daniel: But you see, the process of negation is now negating any value, also. So with negation you can simply see what's not true. Relationship is not something that one does or creates; relationship is a fact of our lives. But usually when we talk of relationship, it's an idea of relationship. The obvious fact of relationship is that everything in this universe is related. It doesn't need to try to relate, it doesn't have to relate; it's not something perpetuated through self or through effort. So when one is living within the framework of self or 'me', then it doesn't seem that it's possible to see the interconnection with all things — not as an idea but as a fact. To perceive the interrelatedness of all life is to also perceive the qualities of energy in different relationships. Only when one perceives the quality of energies in life around one is there a proper response. But without seeing the quality of energy, what you have is an attempt to respond according to an idea.

M: *It's always partial.*

Daniel: And you'll feel the lack, you'll feel the limitation. Through time, this limited approach creates the basis for tragedy or great difficulty. Because through ideas and images we get married, we produce families, we create nations and religions. It's not to say that there is not an underlying energy, something else happening in this universe — it may be. But to the one who is unaware of what is happening, there actually is nothing happening. So what we usually consider to be relationship is a reaction to an emptiness or to a loneliness — something to enhance us, something to give us meaning — whether it's with a mate or with an organization. Relationship, in actuality, is no friction. Each thing, being itself completely, cooperates. I can liken that relationship to the organs in the body — where each organ in the body is doing what it is designed to do — fully, entirely, without friction. And in doing what it is designed to do, each part fulfills a larger function; it moves in conjunction with everything else. There's no reward for that, there's no applause for that, there's no feedback in that.

You can see at this point that actually, relationship happens through aloneness. When one is no longer living in need, no longer looking for enhancement or support structures — because one sees that there's no lack; when one is no longer looking for a mate or an organization or a structure for meaning in life, that understanding is the basis for relationship. Because at that point you're no longer dissipating your energies in pursuit of anything to fulfill you. You realize the absurdity of that. When there is no longer a pursuit, you're now living in a conservation of energy. You're no longer leaving a scar, no longer making a mark, no longer having an effect. Because a dissipation of energies, I can say, was cause. When there is no longer an active cause, in a scattered way, there's no longer an effect — as a scar. So at that point you can say one has come to a stillness. That stillness is the basis for relationship — relationship no longer as an active principle, nor an opposite, passive principle — but relationship as recognition.

M: *I'd like to explore the point at which this happens, this obvious mutation — because of the strength of the conditioning it has to be through a mutation. I was making a picture of this, and it seemed that the only picture I could get was: At what point does* the river make the bank, or the bank make the river? It seems that it's always happening everywhere.

Daniel: There's no actual separation in it, you see. Is stillness love — is love God? Is God light? So with a mind that sees through division, you're taking a step at a time. Stillness is the preparation for perception — which in fact is the preparation for relationship — which is in fact the preparation to perceive light — which in fact is the introduction to God and love. In this we may understand the nature of introduction — that anything moving freely and purely is creative; and that the 'I' or the 'me' center is not creative, but imitative.

M: Is it static?

Daniel: It uses the past to create a future projection, a 'how-to'. So to understand the limit of the 'me' center — to understand that whatever it does, it cannot reach its fulfillment — is a necessary point. Because now we're no longer relying on that forward movement; no longer relying on the structure of pain and pleasure, or reward and punishment, or past and future. When one comes to this point of stillness through that understanding, that stillness is no longer bound by the past, and no longer has a future in the same way — future meaning repetition of the past. Stillness takes place when there is no longer a pursuit, no longer a value system *per se.*

M: It's total.

Daniel: Stillness is a fact — not something I've adopted, not an approach or a technique. Stillness is a fact when I see I cannot move. That stillness is actually the surrender of the thought process as a dominating principle. Stillness is the introduction to helplessness; helplessness is a necessary prerequisite in love. Because in order to explore the quality of life, you must not be able to hurt, you must not be able to impose your standard of behavior.

So obviously, in order to explore something that has no name, that has depth, that is pure, you must be of that quality yourself. If you are of the same quality that you're longing for, in that recognition there is an invitation to go deeper. Where does that journey end? — there is no end, it's ongoing. For the stillness to take place there must be a mutation; to see something never before seen, you must have the capacity to see it. In order to see it, an inner change must take place. As it stands now, you can only see what you are allowed to see according to the known. We cannot see more than what we're taught, what we're conditioned to believe, what we're conditioned to see. When you are moving with that full intelligence, then what you'll see outwardly also seems to have undergone a change.

But the change also has consistency; the change is not some chaotic movement. It is consistent not in that it conforms to a certain structure, but in the sense that it is dependable, reliable — you feel a responsibility, a love of life in which you won't violate anything. When you feel this love for life and you are making this exploration, you see that there is a response. As you move in life now with that quality, people who are on the same frequency will respond. It's not that you are on a mission, or that you are doing anything — it is not 'you' that is doing anything — but when a human being is on a journey in life, there will also be a response to it. It is my feeling that humanity yearns — yearns to be free, yearns to experience and be one with an energy. There is a yearning to return to the source.

M: But it's removed from real urgency.

Daniel: What has taken place is that through time we've developed a very sophisticated form, called the intellect, as a survival instrument. It's not that the survival instrument of the intellect is evil; it's just not enough, it's not fulfilling. So the failure of the ego or the 'me' center can introduce you to the need for something of depth. Repeatedly in our society we are discovering the limitations in what we can create, as individual and and collective egos — we're repeatedly running into our limitations. It's not that we should discard the ego structure or the intellect — it can make a contribution, but it is not all of life. So if I have the potential to live totally, how can I continue to live in this aspect? Once I understand that I can breathe freely, how can I live with any less than that?

When that keenness is there, when that sharpness is there, then many people ask how to go deeper. It's my feeling that simply living — the very miracle, the very charm of life — is the introduction to depth; there's no 'how-to' in it. Even the very things that we feared — the boredom, the emptiness, the doing nothing — now become charged. So life is now a dynamic. And yet you may still take your morning walk or have a simple meal, or do whatever you need to do. We must have the capacity not to be limited by philosophies that we create, by the ideas that we shouldn't do this or we shouldn't do that. We must be able to go into New York City, or Calcutta, or wherever, if in fact it is necessary that we go. So a free being won't avoid — but won't run towards, either.

M: All the disciplines we put upon ourselves don't last too long anyway.

Daniel: They can't, because we're trying to have a total movement out of a very limited aspect. These imposed conditions can't last long.

At one point the 'me' structure was a survival instrument, but now the very survival instrument is threatening. Humankind originally may have needed the 'me' or the identity in order to survive; we were living in a jungle, we were threatened by outer circumstances and situations. But now humankind threatens itself; and now the very thought process, the very center which was designed for survival, is actually turned against itself. The foods it eats, the pleasures and the entertainments it pursues are actually wearing the body down. Conflicting thought is creating great friction, and the brain is being destroyed by it. And the world that we know — which, my feeling is, is alive — is also being destroyed. We're destroying the oxygen, we're destroying our needs, we're destroying life around us. The intellect cannot grasp feeling; it doesn't have a full understanding of life.

M: It goes on emotion and sentiment, and it immediately asks, "What can I do?" The intellect will ask, "What can I do to clean up pollution?"

Daniel: And it can't see not to create it. So the intellect is a doer; it has defined survival as doing. And this is why there is great reaction when it's suggested that we come to rest. Because we associate coming to rest, we associate silence or stillness with donothingism — when the evidence at hand is that all our doing has just gotten us deeper into this quicksand, that in fact doing is the problem; it is humankind's doing and effort that is the great difficulty of our times. So now we look for a way to undo — and to me that's merely doing with a new name; it's an opposite. It still means activity — and it is the activity, the accumulation that turns out to be the violence.

M: No matter how subtle it is.

Daniel: Because we're pressured to move under fear, and any time you move under fear or pressure, any time you move out of loneliness or through crisis, your perception is colored, your view is colored. The only real doing is to come to this point of stillness.

13 August 1979

The Flowering of a Human Heart

Daniel: When I experience pain or sorrow, or the collapse of what I have created, instead of being bowled over by it or destroyed by it, I'm introduced to the need to simply look at the whole quality of my life, at what I've been doing. I see that in fact it is not the environment or the situation out there that is my problem, but how I've been moving with it; I've actually been creating the problem. So, in short, I see at that point that I am the problem, and I create problems in almost everything I do. And my attempt to solve the problem seems to be a way of extending the so-called problem. The problem is not the issue; but it's the issue that introduces me to the fact that I'm a problem-maker. So it's through disaster or through the difficulty of the problem that I'm introduced to myself. And once I realize that, I'm no longer putting the energy of life into creating more problems; I'm now investigating this problem-maker, and why it must create a problem, what its efforts are. So something is now taking place. Instead of pursuing, running after, creating and accomplishing more, acquiring more, the energy that went into that is now available for simply looking at the quality of my own existence — the quality of my thinking, the quality of my information, the quality of my knowledge. And when I examine the quality of my information and my knowledge, I see that they're lacking, that there's still something missing.

So all this has come about only because in the collapse of things, I've realized that a change is necessary; and in enquiring into my body of knowledge I discover I don't know what change is — still change is necessary, but I don't know how to bring it about. And as deeply as I can go, I still don't know how to bring it

The Flowering of a Human Heart   127

about. At that point I discover that I'm helpless — I realize there's a need for change and I cannot create it, bring it about, or produce it. I'm helpless.

But I find that this helplessness is not the death I imagined it to be; it is not the end of the world, it is not the destruction I imagined it to be, I discover that this helplessness is an introduction to a dynamic state. Helplessness no longer is something I fear; helplessness is my introduction to a totally different feeling, a whole new facility, a whole new capacity. Helplessness is the introduction to stillness — when you don't know what to do, and you're no longer running away from that fact, then *you* are now stillness. First you were the problem-maker, and in helplessness you discover stillness; now you are stillness. Stillness now can look, can see the qualities of life. Now you can go deeper. Using stillness as your stepping-stone, the very fact of life around you has now undergone a change. Because in that stillness you can see the different qualities that heretofore you hadn't even noticed.

Now I may come to a point in this enquiry, this inner journey, where I feel that I'm free. I'm no longer bound by the condition or the pressures, by what I thought in the past to be so monumental, so structured. Now I see that it's an illusion, it's an agreement. But I also see it doesn't mean that I violate the conditions of the society; it only means that I'm no longer a prisoner of them. So now the names that I took in the past to be authoritative, or something to rebel against, now become simply functional — mother, and father, and society, and policemen, whatever. They're no longer names or words that threaten me, but they're functional; they allow people, allow me to function in this society. Mother, or father, are names that indicate something functional.

So now I'm no longer at war with the society or the structure around me; I'm not a prisoner. And I can move in it without violating it — I can simply look at them with intelligence. When I've come to that point, I'm not creating any more difficulty; now I'm free to go a bit deeper. But my freedom is now only freedom in relationship. First I've experienced what I would call a personal freedom — and in that freedom I'm responsible not to violate anything. And now I'm introduced further, to the fact that the fuller expression of that freedom is in communication — not to just take my freedom with me and go off somewhere, but now to communicate it. I discover that if I cannot communicate that freedom, I'm not free; I'm stuck. So the further journey is to find a means of communication.

Michael: Could you say that is the first action?

Daniel: Relationship is the movement that comes out of stillness. When one sees a flower, and feels an opening of their own heart, this flower is no longer merely a flower — it is a quality, an expression of beauty; it is contributing beauty.

So I would say that the flowering of a human heart takes place when it realizes the full relationship or connection to life around it. What is this quality in relationship? Because to me it's a very rare thing to be introduced to a relationship that is a flowering, that is deeply a flowering; that is not dependent, that is not grabbing, in which one doesn't want anything. You continue to be your own beauty, your own flower; but in that flowering you're related, and in that relationship flowering is taking place all around you.

So we come to a point where we understand that relationship is essential now to the freedom. But now we've also come to a point where relationship is no longer conditioned; I no longer have an idea of relationship. The flower doesn't pursue; the flower waits to be seen. The flower is there, and those who can appreciate the beauty of the flower also have that quality themselves. So part of communication is that capacity to wait and be recognized.

M: One is there because of what went before, and one's function is what will come. But there's no before and after.

Daniel: Time and space are constructs of thought; in the full reality there is no such thing as this time and space. But in the social reality there is a time and space, and it can be honored. You call something birth and you call something death, but it's all relative; in the larger picture there is no beginning and end as such. You may have an awareness that form is really energy; you may have an awareness that essentially there is no birth and death. But when you live in a society in which these things *are* taking place, and there is a belief that it is taking place, then you need to find a way to navigate in that society without upsetting it. And yet you can find a way to live inwardly, where you're not bound by the concepts. Then time is really an agreement between people. That's all it was originally — an agreement. In order to establish a certain order in our society, we agreed to have time. But what has happened is that we become bound by time, and then we become frightened when we feel bound.

So if you can live in freedom, then you're not bound by the structure. But if you cannot live in freedom, then you will be bound by the structure. But until that intelligence is there, until that realization is there, then we live according to rules and concepts. I do not mean to replace the imposed form with licensed behavior. Intelligence is the only thing necessary. When you can see with intelligence what the need is, you'll find your freedom in everything. And not only will you find your freedom, but in recognizing that freedom only takes place in relationship, you'll provide the basis for freedom in others also. If you have a strong regard for freedom, for sensitivity, for life, you will also provide the room for others to experience what they need to experience. You're not telling them what to do; but they will experience it also.

M: The need is to communicate.

Daniel: The need is transformation — total and full transformation. Through the relationship with a person you may have experienced your whole heart. But if your whole heart is fixed in that position, it's not enough. So the heart must open even further. Through the relationship or through the perception, can you now experience that energy always, and introduce it to all of life? And once you understand that you are what you see, then you see that the neighbors, the family, everyone — are also what you are. Now this is a test in your life. If in fact you have seen that quality of energy, it will make a demand on you that you experience it with everyone sooner or later. Sooner or later, this love that you say you experience is going to demand that you experience it with all of life. You understand that in this relationship is your being, is your heart. In relationship you discover and you experience your full potential as a human being. In this relationship, your heart and your mind are working in coordination, in cooperation with each other.

And if you read today's newspaper, you'll see that there's a dire need. The need is for some intelligent people who are in love. There's a great need for people to experience that love. Only in that love can you experience true relationship. And only when you experience true relationship can you communicate that love, contribute the love you've found, to all of life around you.

15 August 1979

Seeing the Ocean

Michael: I had an image this morning as I was walking — you leave footprints on the sand when you walk on the beach, and the ocean constantly washes them away as soon as you make them. If you never look at your relationship to the ocean — which you could call life — you don't see that your footprints are being washed away, you don't see that you're actually leaving no trace as you go through life. You think you're leaving a trace, you're using this imaginary thing to base your life on, but one look at the ocean tells you everything.

Daniel: But why can't we see the ocean?

M: It's behind us.

Daniel: Why can't we see it? What's lacking? You know, in the midst of this lovely countryside, this lovely day and this lovely home we're in — in the midst of that great grief has taken place, great hurt can take place. Why can't we see the loveliness, why can't we experience it? Why do we have to constantly describe it and make poetry? Because in making poetry we've made it something big, something that we must respect or go towards in a certain sort of bowed way. Why can't we see it for what it is?

So I might go by the ocean and say, "Ah, the ocean, how nice, how beautiful", and then the next day again say "Ah, the ocean, how lovely". But can I see that the people, the fishermen who live there are not saying these things? They live there, going about their business, part of the scene. They are functioning with the ocean — they're in it, they're living with it; they are the ocean. When I'm not living with it, I'm separated from it, I don't see it — what I see is my own description of it. I'm overwhelmed by my own description, and in that I am separate from the ocean; I never experience life fully.

M: *In order for you to be overwhelmed, it has to be separate from you.*

Daniel: So now I come to this point — in order to be anything in relationship to something else, I see that there's a lack of love there. The very desire is separation. Because love doesn't have desire. You can't desire what you are, you can only desire what you're separate from. And that desire brings fantasy and illusion; I embroider now upon the figure. So now in almost every projection, in everything I see, there's a degree of separation; there is space or distance between myself and what I see. When I understand that, I really understand that I haven't seen anything — I'm only seeing my illusion, my description, my projection. No. I must experience the fact. It's essential to me — I need to experience the fact of life.

M: *But I push it away.*

Daniel: This time I'm not pushing it away. I ask this question — why do I need a description before I can see it? Why do I invent desire; why is this separation so important to me that I continue it? What is it?

M: *It's all I've known.*

Daniel: It's all I've known, but now it's not enough — it's not enough. It may be all I know, and you can tell me that all year, but it's still not enough. You tell me I can't love because I don't know how to love; no — I say, I need it. You can tell me that till doomsday, but I still need it. And I ask, why can't I experience it? And I ask that question, really in that yearning, really with that intensity. At that point I understand why the separation has occurred — because to me it wasn't a burning need. I didn't realize it was a burning need. Love or merging was not an option, not a choice. Now I realize it's a need — I can't live without it, I can't excuse it or philosophize it anymore. No more equations will satisfy me.

At that point, again something has changed. The obstacle that existed through your projection no longer exists, because you are focusing your attention on it. Yearning is when you focus your attention on any subject with heart and soul — when you've approached it with a full heart, and with all your heart you need to understand it. You've come to the end; you see that there's no life without the understanding. When with all your heart you need to understand it, then you're focused. When you focus your attention and your intensity in such a way, you discover there is no obstacle. What you see is what you are. When you focus your intensity, through your intensity you see your heart, you see your very being.

M: But it's not unique.

Daniel: There's no name for it. At that point, when you see the so-called ocean, it is no longer ocean to you. You can say it's your bloodstream, it's your breathing, it's your life; it's alive. And that's what you perceive, that's the connection. You experience your life, and you see everything else to be alive also; you experience this life in everything. That experience is a total mutation, a total transformation — when there is absolutely no division at all, and you perceive it.

M: And the body feels the effect; it's one life.

Daniel: There's nothing feeling it anymore.

M: There's no effect?

Daniel: You see, in time there will be; something takes place.

You have this experience where you and what you see are one movement, and you immerse yourself in that experience thoroughly. Now what happens? Does it only exist with the ocean? Because as I'm walking and I'm one with the ocean, and now I come to the boardwalk, and the activity around me — and I say no, I'm looking at the ocean; I only want to see the beauty of the ocean. Then I discover the lack — that my eyes can only see so far. It's still not enough; I can't see that this experience of love excludes nothing.

M: You've discovered something, but it has to be refined.

Daniel: So, that's what I'm introduced to next. I understand then that the further perception is based on complete order in my life. So I come to a point where I can recognize God or love at certain times, in certain people, in certain circumstances — but I have not fully realized that energy in everything. It's not a denial that what I have seen is God, that what I have seen is love; but it's not enough. Because what's the need? It's not that I have a private personal relationship with this energy. It's that what I've experienced in this relationship I must also experience in all relationships. What I've experienced this day I must experience throughout life.

15 August 1979

No Other Life

Daniel: It has been our discovery that if there is enough intensity, the dynamic of needing to understand something will allow us to transcend the form. It's my further premise that a question asked with intensity — with a real yearning or need to understand — creates the response, generates the response; and the resolution or the answer gives birth to something entirely new and fresh. The interviewer therefore has as great a responsibility as does the one interviewed. If the need is to understand something entirely, then one must also yearn for that totally themselves.

Michael: It seems necessary to put aside the past in order for change to take place — but how is one to do that?

Daniel: We have the impression of doing, you know — and so we have the impression that *we* are holding onto the past, and that we can put aside the past. If there is an identity, or a center called 'me', this center has no choice — it *is* the past; and if it attempts to survive, it continues the past. That's what it can do; that's all it knows to do. When I see that in fact the past is happening over and over and over again — that the whole of human history is in fact repetition, and that my personal history is repetition — that very viewing, that seeing, is shedding light on a subject that heretofore had no light in it. That light is the preparation for change. Change is not modification of behavior; change is not getting better; change is not from a fixed point to a fixed point. Change is to understand that the entire structure of thought is present in almost everything that one has done in life, and in fact has not allowed one to experience life first-hand. So I'm not attempting to get rid of it; that's a reaction. The idea that since I've lived in the past and so now must attempt to get rid of the past, is continuity — continuity which takes the form of the doer. The center sees itself as the one who does things; who will now put things right. But the very construct of self is the imbalance; so self is not going to volunteer rightness. Self's only power is continuity; it's a survival instrument. When I see that I am the past — totally see it — that seeing is a dynamic.

M: So that is total.

Daniel: That is what totality means. I understand the ramifications of that, I see it in a glance, I see all of it. I see the family structure, I see the whole societal, religious structure that has come out of it. I see our literature, I see everything, and why it must be; and I see why it continues. In the seeing, I'm introduced to a different quality. What I took to be life, what I took to be necessary, what I've come to expect, I no longer take to be necessary, I no longer expect. When I am no longer pressured to continue in that way, I am introduced to a stillness in my life. That stillness is the basis for the exploration. That stillness is now the basis for actual living.

M: And the future no longer holds any promise.

Daniel: I don't need to be promised anything if in fact I see that I am the universe, that the universe is me. Why do you need to promise me any rewards any more? How can you threaten me, and how can I be pressured in any way?

M: Before this is seen, there is pressure. But if the seeing is a totality as far as the past is concerned, there shouldn't be any more pressure — it shouldn't come in even the subtlest of forms?

Daniel: No, it may. When you're no longer struggling with your individual constructs, and you've come to rest as far as that is concerned, you may now be introduced to subtle constructs, subtle conditions. It may not have anything to do with you personally; it may be the condition of form, it may be the condition of the species, it may be the condition of your race, or whatever. But no pressure that you experience in that regard will be more than your capacity to meet it. So pressure is not the problem, it's the reaction to the pressure.

Questioner: *It seems to be a big concern in our society now — that at the same time we want something, want some experience, we've also been taught that you should do it on your own, see it on your own, experience it yourself; you shouldn't have a guru, or a teacher, or whatever. That seems to be the current philosophy.*

Daniel: When my thirst is great, and my hunger is great, I don't care what form it comes in — as long as it's true. As long as I can see the depth of it, and understand it intelligently, then I can't impose any condition on it, saying it should be this way or that way. So, if you're starving, you're not too concerned who gives you the food. Your concern is that it's real food. If you're in great need, and you understand that need — you're yearning for something real — that very yearning will generate the response. When the yearning is intense, the recognition is also part of the yearning.

So let's not get caught on the idea of my own, or your own, or guru, or teacher, or whatever it is. Guru, by its very nature, doesn't mean threat; it means response. Guru implies relationship, a relationship of softness and intelligence — a real yearning on the parts of the people concerned to understand life first-hand, to see it. When one is completely tired of this violence and disturbance in their life, and they have a dynamic need to understand, to live, guru is the response to that dynamic need. If that is taking place for you, then there is no problem with guru. But if guru is some condition that you've created to continue your difficulty — something that supports you, something that constantly allows you to maintain a certain condition — then that's not guru you're talking about, that's not the original quality. What you call guru then is a crutch. And that crutch, to a person who is not crippled, creates illness.

Obviously there has been great deception in the past. But we've never realized what that great deception means — it also means that my seeking, my longing isn't pure. So that the guru is not a clear guru also indicates that a disciple is not a clear disciple; that a teacher is not a full teacher also indicates that a student is not full. So if you as an individual can devote yourself to understanding what it is you need in your life — simply, wholeheartedly — the very formulation of the need will also show you the way.

Questioner: Could you make a clear distinction between the one movement, of creating one's own reality out of desire or out of limitation — and the other movement, of generating the answer out of a question which is pure yearning?

Daniel: You see, we all have the capacity to invent a reality. We can invent a reality out of our thought, out of our memory; and through desire, which stems from a center, stems from an idea of self. But that invention will also require you to support it, to maintain it, to be worried about it.

Q: Because you're separate from it still.

Daniel: Because it obviously is your invention — it has nothing to do with life, it has nothing to do with real creativity. And any time you impose a condition through desire, the very center of that condition is fear; the very center of your desire is fear. You'll have to maintain it, and in order to maintain it, you'll have to know more fear and conflict.

How is that compared to an actual act of creation that does not come out of fear? An act that takes place through recognition — as a response to a need — will not know fear. So again, the question goes into how to understand when your reality is an invention of thought and when it's an experience of creativity. Time — time will introduce us to the fact. The fact is eternal; it doesn't need anyone's support to maintain it. So something that is real is eternal. But something that comes out of the 'me' state, the ego state, something that is created by me personally — for my

No Other Life 139

personal satisfaction — will always be limited, and therefore always threaten me. So in time, what is not true will collapse. What is created or generated by love or intelligence will not collapse. Love's creation is eternal.

Questioner: Doesn't one have to be — almost pure in a sense, to even come to that need or see that need?

Daniel: Well, it seems that if you're to recognize something straightaway, it means that there is no greater pressure. It means that you're not distracted; it means that you're free to recognize it. If you would call the freedom to look purity, then yes — I would say you need to be pure. If you say that the need to love requires a clarity, a directness, yes — I would say it does require that. So I don't mean the purity that comes through effort, or as an act of will. I mean purity that comes only through recognition, a purity that comes only out of surrender. I'm not talking about an act of will or effort. I'm talking about the essential recognition that what you're engaged in, what you're doing, cannot allow you to experience life; the basic recognition that whatever you do, you cannot realize the essential qualities in life. There's no way out.

So we must be able to distinguish what we need. If you can distinguish what you need, the terms are not overwhelming. If you understand what you're looking for in the simplest way, then there will not be a struggle with the response. If you don't understand what you're looking for, then you're subject to all the pressures. But the understanding of what you need will free you from the pressure. And then if you do understand what you need, you're ready; the receptivity is there.

So the receptivity depends on where you stand, what ideas you have. If in fact you're not imposing a condition, then you can just view life as it is. On the surface we can see that children are a product, a reflection of the quality of the parents; you can just see it in the resemblance, you can see it in the attitude. And as it's reinforced in the actual living condition at home and in school, you see that the children will start to take on the traits of the society and the family. It seems that they are born with receptivity, with a genetic predisposition for that. And once further reinforcement has taken place, this crystallizes; it appears to harden. Now there are some people who apparently have not been exposed to so much; whose point of view has not been so shaped that for one reason or another they've experienced a relative freedom in their life. They're ready to see the fact, they're eager to.

But I'm not speaking to special people or unusual people. What I've mentioned here is not something unavailable to the average human being. I'm speaking to the person who has experienced the hurts and the sorrows of everyday living, who has a degree of sophistication, who has accumulated information or has received an education in our society — who whether working in an office or reacting to the social structure, is just daily feeling frustration; and in feeling the frustrations has come to somewhat understand the artificiality of our existence — the constructs, the pressures. It seems to me that the future lies in this person's hands. And the complete collapse is in his hands also. Because obviously the trauma is not so great that one cannot hear; and yet one is receiving enough feedback and comfort in the society that there is a great incentive to continue the system. So this being who is forced to straddle two worlds is the one who must hear; this is the one who must see, this is the one who holds life in his hands.

In the past, we've attempted to hold up any person who has made a breakthrough in their life as someone special, and in that special quality we've kept them at a distance; we've adored them or prayed to them or admired them. And you can only do that if someone is separate from you — someone who you view out there or up there, from where you are, down here. In that construct, there's a great separation. In that admiration, you're not compelled to understand your need.

So we can have the opinion that in time and space, some day, I will achieve the capacity to be like that — and our misery continues, our sorrow continues, our hurt continues. But when the possibility of a simple human being achieving his fullness, just achieving the capacity to touch upon something vast, when it's seen in front of you — when there's no mystique, no separation, when it's demystified — then you're confronted with a real challenge in your life. If the common human being can experience fullness and love without the cliché, without the romantic images, but actually; if the simple person can in one stroke put down the accumulated burden of history in front of him, and in one moment touch upon divinity or greatness in his daily activity — without any background, without special tools or acquired discipline, but just with a simple yearning to experience it fully, a realized need to touch upon something vast in life — at that point, if you see that, what is your challenge? So to me, the greater need is that it takes place in the simplest way. If you yourself feel the need to touch upon this quality in life, the intensity of that need is the receptivity required to experience it. That to me is our challenge.

M: I see that freedom may mean the loss of all I've accumulated — the thought of it brings me fear. Is fear, or is sorrow and pain necessary for understanding?

Daniel: Fear is not a foe or an enemy, it's an indication. If you understand what pain or fear indicates, then it seems to me that you no longer need to feel continued pain; pain has done its job. If you recognize that, then pain and sorrow is obviously not a lifestyle. It only takes place because you're not conscious, you're not aware, you're not available to the needs in life. If you've taken care — if pain has introduced you to the need for order in your life — then you've also stepped out of the need for sorrow and pain.

So sorrow and pain are only necessary if you refuse to wake up. But let's not make a philosophy of sorrow and pain being necessary — no. If you think it's necessary, it will continue to be. If you discover that you don't know what is necessary, what form it must take — but that your need, your formulated need is to live, is to love, is to understand it all — then you prepare for that.

M: May I ask if the preparation takes any form as we know it — definitely not the form of thought — but is there a particular realm this preparation is in?

Daniel: You see, I have an experience where I'm touched by an essential quality; I understand that there is a life, there is a fullness, there is an experience that is just out of reach. And once I understand that it exists, that it is available, and I'm not experiencing it — at that point I am starting to understand my need.

M: Just a simple fact.

Daniel: Just a simple fact. Now the simple fact introduces me to the need for greater preparation. What is greater preparation, factually — not an idea of greater preparation?

M: It's actual learning.

Daniel: And learning simply means that in the past I have carried too much information and too many opinions, too many ideas of *what is* before I could learn; I couldn't learn anything. So now my need is to learn, my need is to experience or feel first-hand.

So now what is my preparation, when I need to learn? My first preparation is not to create any impediments, any obstacles. My first preparation is to establish order in my social existence, so that I am free to experience. So depending on your actual circumstance in life — whether you've created a family, children, a home; whether you have gurus, or teachers, or whatever; whether you're fearful of not having enough money, whether you have a job that is pressuring you, or even feel content in; whether you've defined yourself by some talent, such as writing or painting — once you see what you've created in your life, you see that in order to carry on in this journey, in order to experience first-hand, you must be free to go. Then the freedom to learn means that you've put your affairs in order.

M: There's no static circumstance here, though.

Daniel: No — you must also introduce this quality into your life in everything. I may see that I thought I was a writer, I thought I was a painter, I thought I was a mother, I thought I was a father — and relatively it's true; it is a function. But now I see that I also have the capacity to create an identity out of it. So I identify myself as the writer, or as the painter; and now writing and painting are no longer just an expression of harmony, they are now difficulty and pressure. I see that I was the mother or the father, and it's functional — you're growing up with someone who may physically need your help. But psychologically, the idea of mother or father can be greatly distracting; you can have so many expectations, and fears, and hopes, and dreams. You're so preoccupied with your construct that you're not free to live. If you realize that your need is to live wholly and fully, then you're able to ascertain what is actually necessary, and what is your construct. There's a tremendous freedom, a tremendous release in that, to understand what is the fact — where it is physically a function and a responsibility on your part, and where it is an invention that comes out of your psyche.

So what you've done in that moment is eliminate pain and fear in your life. That's what it means to put life in order — you're no longer subject to the pains and pressures, because you no longer want anything. You have a great need, and in order to realize that need, you're putting your affairs in order. So that means that you're no longer pressured by the labels, you're no longer pressured by the current ideas, you're no longer looking for romance, you're no longer dealing in seduction; you're not involved in it all. You're not putting it down, you're not even involved with the whole argument of it being correct or incorrect; you see what the need is, and the need introduces you to a further need to prepare. That preparation will allow you to go deeper in life.

Without that preparation, we're not free to go. We want to experience love or God or whatever, and we think that it's something that we have to pursue or acquire; we don't understand that the receptivity is not there, the capacity to recognize the existence of love hasn't emerged in us yet. We don't recognize it because we're not prepared for it. We have so many things that call us that we can't recognize the reality. So the preparation is the preparation for reality. And one who can prepare is real himself.

Questioner: Is already realized —

Daniel: Yes. Is there. What you're looking for, you're actually experiencing already. But without that recognition, without that preparation, you must always pursue it in the future — some time, some day. When you don't realize it, you hope for it. So hope is the avoidance of recognition; you would not hope for something you're experiencing. If you were in love, you would not hope for love. If you had discovered the essential need and quality in life, you would obviously not need hope. So hope is an indication that you're not real, you're not alive, you're not full.

Questioner: It's really simple in a sense.

Daniel: Simplicity is the need also, you see.

M: But we get caught up in a part-time approach, which implies an incomplete need — I see that.

Daniel: We don't realize the larger need. When it's happening in a part-time way, let it indicate to us that we're part-time people. When it's happening to us in a part-time way, there's something further in that; it is the indication to go deeper. When I experience something in this room, and I go to my own room and I don't experience it any longer, then instead of going into depression and fear, can I understand that the need now has changed a bit — the need now is to introduce it into my total life, not to only have it in certain circumstances. When one has no other life than realization, then that life is a constant introduction to further realization.

20 August 1979

A Life Beyond Hurt

Daniel: In looking back, I find that hurt and pain has been a consistent quality throughout life. And I also find that I am seen through that hurt. When the people that I have hurt hear my name or see me, they recall that hurt, they see me through that past memory; and I find I tend to do the same thing. When I see that quality, I make a discovery in my life that in doing what I felt I wanted to do, or needed to do, I've hurt others, and I've been hurt by others. And in simply seeing that, I understand that a life of hurt or pain is not life, and that when this occurs in relationship it's obviously not relationship; the relationship can't blossom, we can't learn anything more. We're stuck in the idea of hurt, we're fixed according to the form of hurt. And my yearning is to be free, my need is to be free of it, to step out of this absurdity, this mediocrity of living in hurt all the time, of lashing out and being hit back. I see that it's not life.

I need to experience something of validity, something of quality — something that is dynamic. There's no longer room for hurt, there's no longer room for blame or complaint in your personal existence. At that point, life is a responsibility — a responsibility to be free, to be intense, to be full. And when you have that much concern for the life that you're living, then you're introduced to the concern for life in general. If you see that it's very important that the life you're living is free — by its very nature must be free — then in providing your own freedom, you're also concerned about the freedom of the life around you. So when you no longer exist in hurt personally, you're no longer hurting.

Now, when you're no longer hurting, what does that mean in

relationship to your past; to the people you have hurt, and have been hurt by? My feeling is that in order for that past hurt to continue, it needs to have fuel added to it, it needs another incident and another incident; in fact, the very attempt to undo it may also be a reminder which serves to continue it. So it's not that I'm caught up in a construct of undoing anything, or doing something; I see at this point that I am not going to participate in continuing any form of behavior; I need to be free of it. That love of freedom, that love of life, is no longer providing continuity to the past hurt. That this past hurt can live on itself without the continuity does not seem possible. The hurt, if it's a psychological hurt, needs continuity, needs reinforcement, needs fuel added to its fire to continue on as hurt. If in fact a radical change has happened in your life, where you're no longer able to hurt yourself or those around you, then the past psychological hurts that you have inflicted no longer have the fuel necessary to continue. And when you're no longer bound by the past, you're no longer projecting the past into the future, you see. You're not bound by a past, and you no longer have a dictated or programmed future. Now life is a dynamic.

Michael: For one — but what about the others involved?

Daniel: If life is a dynamic for one, it will not be limited to one. Because the next step in that dynamic quality is relationship, a full, pure, true relationship — not based on any of these psychological prisons, not carrying a psychological burden or support structure; not a relationship based on fear or loneliness, not one of convenience.

So obviously, if none of these things are taking place, one has discovered individual aloneness. This full individual aloneness introduces you to a relationship of aloneness — but aloneness as a connected state, aloneness with the channel open, aloneness in realizing your full individual potential. And then in realizing that potential, you're introduced to the greater need of full and pure relationship. That relationship is the further introduction to all of life; it is no longer revolving around a personal construct.

A Life Beyond Hurt   147

M: *Can the past be used as a tool if two parties are both receptive to that exploration?*

Daniel: Anything can be utilized if it no longer creates this attachment or fear. So the past can be viewed if you understand what you're doing. But usually when we look at the past, we react to it, and therefore we're bound by it. But if the past can be seen without reaction, surely it can be looked at, and utilized as a guideline.

When the intense human being discovers this state of full stillness, stillness can view this earth, stillness can proceed. The very proceeding through the stillness is an introduction to all the qualities of existence. Those who are also able to carry on in this journey will come along, or also realize their need.

So relationship, to me, is a realized need; and the realized need can only manifest when one is no longer creating impediments, when one is no longer revolving around certain issues, when one is no longer creating problems and then attempting to solve them. Relationship is then a full conservation of one's energy. It's not that you have to work it out or make it better, or do this or that to maintain a relationship. Relationship *is* conservation of energy; it is a realized fact. When one realizes the fact of relationship, it is no longer mired or bogged down in this psychological mud, this sort of quicksand that constantly needs a feedback and reassurance; obviously anything that needs reassurance and feedback will collapse when it's not forthcoming. Any relationship of dependency, when in fact there is no need to be dependent, will always suffer the results of any artificial psychological quirk, or limitation, or pressure; it will also suffer the pain, the problems, the difficulties of that pressure.

So we come to associate effort with fulfillment. We've therefore come to feel that pressure and difficulties are essential to life. We've come to think that sorrow or pain is a necessary ingredient in our existence; and we've also come to think that the moods, the ups and downs, are part of life. So we're now in a ludicrous situation — and I say ludicrous because fullness, harmony, complete intensity, seems to be the abnormal, seems to be the unusual. And the norm is sorrow and pain, discomfort, pressure, psychological burdens, clinging, moods, ups and downs — this is considered to be the norm, what life should be or needs to be. So we're able to excuse our difficulties by demonstrating that everyone is experiencing it. I discover in my life that it's an imposed condition, not a reality. I've imposed that condition, and through that imposition I receive enough feedback to continue. That's not life.

Life waits, intelligence waits, love waits; it simply waits to be recognized. You can only recognize that quality of life when you're no longer dissipating your energy in the so-called issues; when you're no longer susceptible to the pressures of the day, when you're no longer in pursuit of relief from the tensions that you've created in your life. So, when one is no longer engaged in this dissipation of energy, when one sees the need, conservation of energy is taking place in that perception. Conservation of energy *is* the necessary state, *is* the actual stillness, *is* meditation. Conservation of energy is when one is meditating on the feeling, is aware of what they're feeling, when they no longer have an available outlet. When there is no longer an available outlet, because you recognize it's a conditioned outlet, then you are alone with that feeling. That's the dynamic state.

M: I see that if you just stay with this feeling in that simplicity, this seems to be the key.

Daniel: You can only stay with it when it's choiceless — when you're without choice. You've come to a point in this exploration where you see that your entire life is exploration. It is not something that you arbitrarily do; it is something that you need to understand and express. It's your life.

21 August 1979

The Child of Intelligence

Daniel: In the midst of a relationship, you may see that you're in trouble — that someone responded to your romantic image, your performance, and you're required to continue the performance in order to maintain the relationship. If it takes place in that way, if you wake up in the midst of having created something — even though the creation may have come out of habit or fear — the waking up, or the understanding of what you're doing at that moment allows something else to enter. It introduces light into the relationship — you can see it boldly and clearly. Whatever the initial action — whether it came out of fear or loneliness — if it is no longer fear or loneliness, there's no longer continuity. Without this continuity the relationship will find its level, you see. As long as the continuity is there, you can't see the actuality. But if you wake up in the midst of what you've created, you're no longer putting out that forward energy; you're no longer continuing in the same way. You understand that something is quite delicate, something is very fragile, and you approach it in that very careful way, very concerned way. That concern is actually the introduction of light — to enlighten, to turn the light on, you see. When you turn the light on in anything, any relationship, you're really seeing it for the first time. Seeing it for the first time, you'll be very careful. That carefulness won't allow any more violence to take place.

What has happened when you have introduced light, when you have introduced a concern for freedom, a concern for human values into the relationship? The partner in the relationship is no longer defending themselves, they're no longer creating an opposite movement, they're no longer in reaction themselves. The reaction needs two; a tug of war needs two. So the one who sees the game, the violence, the hurt, is the one who lets go. In that letting go the other person cannot continue very long in reaction. When the energy in the relationship is no longer going into performance, then that conservation of energy, I would say, is the basis of relationship — when there's a mutual concern for life, when there's the mutual capacity to see, to understand, to feel. In that there can't be any fear, or loss, or anything like that. When there is no longer dissipation of energy, but a movement together — and the moving together is not based on or revolving around an idea or projection, but is an actual quality that can be felt and experienced by both; it's no longer a support structure, or a leaning on each other, but a union of two beings that feel free, and in that freedom merge — the child that comes out of that merger is relatively pure, in the sense that there will be very little genetic conditioning. The parents who have a certain respect or a real concern for freedom and warmth in their own lives will also express that warmth and feeling for freedom in all their activities. In relationship to the youngster they will also provide that quality — not according to any value system or principle, but just in recognizing the personal need in themselves for freedom; their every action will indicate that concern. I feel that the child will also express that quality, without a how-to.

Questioner: The question may come up as to how set the genes really are — the theory is that the genetic conditioning we're born with is the way it is — certain basic tendencies are set. But that also may be an assumption. So, as many people have asked, when you have already conditioned something or someone in a way that you may even see to be incorrect, can it be undone at that point, or is it set? To what extent are these genes still responsive, still affected by what's happening in our lives?

Daniel: I see that there's only one unchanging quality in life, and that would be the real essence of life. And this essence or source has no name, has no attributes; it has no quality, no fixed form. It's pure. Now around that, we have names, we have fixed forms

— but these forms also have the capacity to change. They appear to be fixed; but even the conditioned genes are essentially habit. And any being alive cannot live in habit very long, if he actually experiences the habit, experiences that in fact he *is* living in habit; the full impact of that perception *is* the change. Whatever the condition, whatever the situation, the perception allows change to take place. In fact, the whole genetic structure is a product of thought. It *is* defined, it *is* limited, it *is* the past, it is an extension of the past. Being an extension of the past, it's also an imposed condition.

Q: *Then it doesn't mean that we're limited by it.*

Daniel: We're limited by it as long as we don't understand that it's taking place. The full understanding of what is taking place is also the release. So it may appear that as we were, we will continue to be; but the recognition of that limitation is also the release. It only appears that we're handcuffed to the past; it appears that we must repeat the past into the future, and that we are tied to it. But when a being in fact sees the handcuffs, he is no longer bound by them.

Q: *Then you see that the past and the future don't exist anyway.*

Daniel: Then the past no longer creates a pressure. Then the past is just something of information; it no longer imposes a condition. Then you see that time is basically an agreement, not a yoke around your neck.

Q: *As you have been saying, when one sees that this is what I've been and therefore this is what I must continue to be, usually that brings fear — fear that there's no way out of it, that it's a conditioned situation that one is bound by.*

Daniel: Once there's a reaction to fear, that in fact is the continuity — the reaction to fear. So, I can only understand the whole condition when there is no way out of it. I will not recognize the need as long as I have an outlet psychologically. The psyche seeks to continue, and so the psyche creates this fear, this anticipation of pain in order to avoid the perception.

Q: But must this perception come through hopelessness? In other words, when one really sees that there's no way out, usually the movement is into a hopelessness.

Daniel: Which is a way out.

Q: It's a different method of escape. But from what we're saying, sometimes it seems that we must go through a true hopelessness, and only through that can surrender occur. But when hopelessness is seen through fear, some may feel that the only way out is through some awful black hole. In the past, it seems that many people just haven't been able to swallow that. Why should they step into that?

Daniel: Sure, why should they — unless we really have an understanding, somewhere deeply, that the unknown is not the problem, the known is the problem. You see, what we call the unknown is actually our projection — it's really the known. We project a quality called the unknown. The problem is the continuity, not the dimension beyond continuity; the problem is that we continue to carry on the tradition of the past, and in fact we haven't lived to our potential, we haven't experienced an essential quality. That essence is never a threat, but for a mind that is seeking to continue, to dominate, anything real must be threatening. So we come to think that the reality is the problem, when in fact the difficulty is that we're handcuffed, that we've imprisoned ourselves in time.

So you cannot invite someone to step into what they may presume to be a black hole, or just a basically bad deal. Mind will always move to better itself, to get more; mind is an instrument for survival. It seeks any outlet or channel for survival. The mind must see — not in hopelessness, but directly and clearly — that it has no choice. When in the midst of relating to your child, you

The Child of Intelligence 153

may impose a condition, and in that moment you can see, twenty years from now, the reaction that must come out of it. In that moment with the child you can also see your relationship to your father, and how you felt. So at that moment, you've just seen the whole movement of time. When you see the resemblance so thoroughly, you're choiceless.

Q: *You'll never discover it through psychological research.*

Daniel: No, because in a moment of crisis or pressure, the psychological, and all scientific and religious research will collapse for you. Because it is something that you've acquired, it is not something that is you — actually, entirely. The acquisition is not very strong. Without the support for it, it collapses very quickly.

Questioner: *When we are dealing with children, how is the conditioning that we've been speaking about here involved?*

Daniel: You know, at one point the ego crystallizes. So we can't rely on the idea of child any longer, you see. In this instance we could say that the child is one who has no separate ego, or separate opinion, or separate social experience to such an extent that there's a need for reaction.

What I'm suggesting now is that actually what we're left with is understanding the need — in our own lives. In understanding the need in our own lives, we're introducing that element around us. If you understand the need in your own existence for freedom, for full expression, not to have these imposed limitations, at the same time that you're growing together with a child, then in understanding the need in yourself, you're also providing for that quality in the youngster.

It's not really different with an eighteen or twenty-one year old, except there's a question that you've introduced time. When the child is physically dependent on you — actually, not under an artificial construct, but actually — the umbilical cord still exists, you see. It exists because there's an actual need; so what you are is also being passed on, conveyed. But now you have a child who is eighteen or twenty-one, who physically doesn't have that need, but may actually have a great need to experience an opening of their heart, a flowering of their being. If you understand that need in yourself, in time that will also be communicated. But it's a question of time.

Q: It seems then to be a question of education.

Daniel: With that you have to be careful. The education is no problem, but you must understand that you can't simply rely on education — that education is there as a tool for real understanding. If you're not pressured yourself, it won't be overwhelming, because then you understand that education is a recommendation. It's really quite flexible. You understand that the world doesn't collapse if the report card says C or D or whatever; you just understand what is being said in it. My feeling is that a child who has the opportunity to explore fully will also have the capacity to just breeze right through most of these things. If the studies are not an imposed condition, then you've taken the pressure out of it; you understand it's a suggestion, a societal suggestion, that's all. You're not involved in achievement, you're not involved in accumulation or anything like that. When you're not after the rewards in the society, and you're not afraid — when you've come to terms with the so-called big issues in the society, of death, and life, and love, and romance; you understand what they are and you're moving through them — then you will also not impose a condition on the youngster. Then you'll serve as a light for the youngster; whatever the imposed condition in the society, whatever the pressures in the society, there will be one place that they look where they can see light. If you've experienced that light, they'll also express that light themselves. But if the pressure does exist, then you'll understand that your experience still isn't perfect, it's not full.

Questioner: *And yet children seem to need a fixed form in order to function, because they are always confronted by the school sys-*

tem, by the grandparents, by everything else that they need to know. They are almost demanding a fixed form.

Daniel: Sure, that's going to be our challenge in this society — that you may experience a full movement that you can call freedom, not be bound; but you'll also have to communicate that quality to people who are living in fixed forms, who are living traditionally, or according to something. And what is called the norm in the society, you may experience to be actually the great difficulty. But that fixed form living is the norm in the society.

Q: Isn't it almost as if one is preparing them or suggesting that they live in the way the parents have found to be best?

Daniel: That's to create the basis of opposites, though. You know, once you impose, once you even suggest any one condition — to be some way — that way is always a reaction to something else. The only way is in something that's not in opposition to anything else, that stands on its own. So, to get in an airplane and to order your food, you can say you're a vegetarian; but to think of yourself as a vegetarian, you see, is to really impose a condition in your life. But if you in fact see that what you call meat is not food, it's simply not food for you — if you perceive that — then eating vegetables or some other food is not in reaction to that condition. It stands on its own, it has intelligence on its own. So, I would say that it is not necessary to impose a condition on the child called vegetarianism, or any of these value systems.

Q: I might not, but when they go to school and the diet is different, that affects the child — it causes a sort of isolation.

Daniel: Okay, so that will happen; and it seems to me that's an essential learning experience. You know, life is going to intercede, we're going to be affected by it; we can't just say that the societal structure has no meaning. We're being challenged by it, and it's forcing growth, it's forcing a greater understanding. A sensitivity that exists only in the family structure, or in the home, is a limited sensitivity. The challenge is going to be to communicate that quality of your existence wherever you are in the society. So, some party in the relationship has to understand what is the real value, what is the real quality; because without understanding the real quality, you have two ego structures pulling their own way, according to their own value systems. Some member in the relationship must understand the essential quality — not his or her way, but what is the fact. Life will always move to the fact at one point; it must. When the whole structure of psyche collapses, the fact will be exposed. The essential energy doesn't change. When you are no longer imposing a condition of psyche or thought, when you're no longer confined to time and space and the projection into the future, based on the past, what is real will emerge or flower.

So if in fact in the relationship with anyone, with the child, with the society, you are able to see the fact — not your condition, but the fact — in understanding the need for a factual existence, you're left with the only true expression; that's waiting. Now waiting may verbalize, waiting may simply be a fixed state, it may be anything. But inside yourself you're waiting for the real quality to express itself. If you're living at home, and you see the circumstance around you is just caught up in so many ideas, so many habits, and you experience a need for great freedom, then experience that need so deeply that in fact the outer circumstance responds to it. The response is not based on your forward movement or your pressure then. Because it is always important that what you communicate is real, is not an artificial condition. And it's very important that what you communicate to the youngster is not theory, but is something that you actually experience, that you feel to be really important; that your well-being depends on it, and the child's well-being depends on it — it is not something that you're toying with.

So when you are in fact indicating to the child that a respect for life is necessary, it's only because you experience deep inside yourself that it is necessary. There needs to be a real passion in it, you see; because otherwise what we are is the product of these contrived circumstances — and we will bring up children accord-

The Child of Intelligence   157

ing to this theory or that idea. What we've done in that is to make a product, or some sort of thing out of the child that we're going to relate to.

Obviously, the need is always to look into your heart, to experience that quality in yourself. And in experiencing that quality, you can see the real need. It doesn't mean that the child will not go through stages, but even in passing through these stages — all the stages of humankind — that grace still can be conveyed, that grace can be experienced. It doesn't mean that the youngster won't grow up, won't participate in the activities in the society. But it does mean that the youngster has experienced light, or grace in her life, and can see it. Now, how it will express is unknown. But if you've experienced it, you can be sure that those who are moving with you will experience it somehow, some way. The energy that you experience is transforming you, and it's also a transforming energy around you. A transformed being is also a transforming being — but not through effort. And you are not afraid of asking for something, not afraid of expressing something very clearly and concisely. When you have touched that quality in yourself, there's no longer a fear of imposing a condition; you know it can't be. Because it is not your condition, it is not your personal expression that you're trying to impart. And you'll only move according to the person's capacity to respond. You'll only move according to the youngster's capacity to receive it. When you're feeling your heart, you also understand the capacity of the other person to receive.

30 August 1979

The Social Issue

Daniel: We live in a time in which we don't seem to have any purpose; there's a great restlessness, a great pressure to find something to do, to identify with, to give life meaning. So in this you may find movements of all sorts occurring in our society, and one form of activism will be social protest over certain issues in our society — nuclear energy, civil rights, women's rights, children's rights, sexual rights, and so on. Just reading in the newspaper, one notices the brutality that can take place when people are looking for entertainment or distraction. When one is living a life without meaning, or without substance, one loses sensitivity; and then sexuality seems to become a great act of violence — it's no longer even an attempt to find relief. And as with sexuality and entertainment, this social concern is one of the highest forms of identity available in the society. It's not to say that the activity itself — the marching against injustice, the demonstration to save a whale or stop the killing of the seal — has no meaning or substance; obviously on the face of it you can see that there is great social imbalance. To have to slaughter in order to be fashionable — obviously there's no arguing with that. To destroy the air, to destroy the sea, to destroy the land in order to fuel the automobiles, or to heat the homes — there seems to be an obvious imbalance in it. But to me it's not the issue that is the problem; it's the imbalanced, restless human beings who are constantly looking for an issue to define themselves by. Because my feeling is that a dynamic being who has a sense of purpose — who has touched a quality in life, a real essence, an undeniable fact or truth in life — can plainly see what is a real issue that has substance, and what is a waste of energy.

So a being that is looking for an issue to continue his behavior will seize upon anything, and again attempt to find continuity in that issue — and in the long run create more scars and more damage. In that I would say generally that the victim and the victimizer are one movement, they create each other, they're made for each other; that the marcher and the manager of the establishment seem to be interconnected; that the existing government, and those who attempt to overthrow it and install their own form, are part and parcel of each other — they're connected, and they continue the disturbance. Because what is taking place in that is that mind is finding a means of continuity — whether through ownership or through overthrowing the ownership. The disturbance finds a way to continue, and this disturbance can call itself civil rights, marching to better mankind, finding progress through capitalism or through a sane energy policy.

So we live in an age of great restlessness, and therefore live in an age of issues — traumatic issues, great issues. These issues will also come and go. It all ties in; the question of restlessness, or not having a meaning in life, takes us into so many areas — takes us into the family, takes us into spirituality, takes us into politics. Is there any thing real in it? Once the disturbance is there — and the disturbance is almost like an infection which seeks to continue — then it takes over almost everything in life.

Questioner: Yesterday we were talking about the symbol of the hurricane — when you look at the whole earth, the storm is a manifestation of a redistribution of energy. But as it moves across the world, it's moving through our constructs — we're all either worried or not worried; it gives us an issue, gives us something to project ourselves onto.

Daniel: There's almost a direct evidence that the universe is going on without our participation.

Q: So what's seen as threat is usually, actually, already the energy trying to regain its own balance.

Daniel: Yes — without understanding the real need, we then attempt to regain a balance only through the thought process, which is an artificial construct. So what is balance? Balance is the capacity to see what is going on. Without that fundamental perception, it's not balance that we're talking about, it's our idea — we're actually only asserting ourselves.

So we have evidence at times that there's a universe out there that is happening. We have direct evidence at times that we don't know very much about what's going on around us. Without realizing the essential quality, we're always on the defensive, always defending ourselves, or projecting a defense necessary — against society, against the universe. So then life is a threat, and we live in this constant fear. This fear then goes out into the world and constructs, directs, develops; and through its constructs and developments it finds an identity, tries to maintain an identity. And obviously the only way to maintain that identity, that construct, or artificial circumstance, is through great effort. But since it is artificial, you'll need pressure and stress. Once that stress and pressure has taken hold, there's also a demand to maintain the artifact — the artifact also meaning religion, meaning race, creed, tribe, city, country, nationality; you can see the great pressure now to maintain the artificial construct.

Now we live in a society in which the very energy necessary to its running is pressure. The society runs on stress and pressure, and the reward that one receives is a temporary respite from pressure — a vacation, or entertainment of one sort or another, or an identity. Once you come to think that this social construct is necessary, then you'll also come to think that the great issues are social issues. You see, mankind, coming to think that man is the center of the universe, also thinks that the issues raised are the essential issues in life. So, if you say that the issues are in fact not issues at all — just propaganda, just a construct — it appears that you're attacking the very standards, the very substance in human beings' lives. Without the issue to identify with, I'm nothing. So it is considered very important that the religion, the nationality continue; very important that the idea of self continue and survive — from family to family, from community to community. Anything of clarity, any universal, any softness, is viewed as a threat.

What have we created in living a life of stress and pressure? Everything we touch also has stress and pressure in it; everything that we've created also has this quality in it. So, it's my feeling again that the universe is happening without us. Something that is real cannot be perceived by an unreal human being, by someone who is preoccupied with their constructs. And when the energy in the being is going into support systems and maintenance of this construct, there is simply no capacity to understand anything of quality. We mentioned the other day that the child, from infancy on, is constantly given something to do — the constant feeding, the constant game-playing, the constant drive, this desire to have the whole day occupied with activity. And then there's great fear when one experiences nothing to do. It's called boredom — and immediately something is supplied. You take this into so-called adulthood, and what we have is that same great fear of emptiness or boredom; the society is constructed around it. A being is never left alone, never experiences a quality of aloneness. The very idea of aloneness creates great fear. Then the word aloneness equals loneliness, and there's great pressure again in that. If you even imagine yourself alone for a moment, you have to give it a name, you have to give it some purpose, create a whole structure around it also.

We are afraid to experience anything real, anything of substance in life. And without the recognition of that fear, without the recognition of the real need, life is taking place without us. It's happening — life is happening around us, the universe is happening around us. All these qualities that we think we're looking for, that we're seeking, are there in front of us, are there inside us — and cannot be felt, experienced or perceived by a being who is pursuing his thoughts, running after constructs, living in fear. To me that fear and that clinging to the illusion is the basis of humanity's pain, humanity's illness; the basis of war. Two ideas clashing, two thought-forms destroying each other will be the basis of war between people — whether in the household called family, or on the battlefield between governments.

Activity is always war; action is never war. Activity is a movement without understanding; it is a physical attempt to dissipate energy through identification. Full action is without any identification at all — it's a complete movement without friction; it leaves no residue. A life lived in full action is a life of meditation.

4 September 1979

One Need in Life

Daniel: The mere recognition of the essence creates a transformation. Because what can recognize essence except essence itself? So the challenge in life now would be the ability for a being to feel deeply, discover deeply, and express that feeling and discovery in action. There have been quite a few beings who have approximated that, who have come close to an essence. The failure in the past, if there is such a thing as failure, is the limitation in expression — not the failure in realization, but the inability to express that realization entirely and thoroughly. Full communicating means to understand fully and thoroughly what this energy is, to immerse oneself in it.

Questioner: But isn't the energy itself the expression — not that the energy has an expression?

Daniel: I would say the essence and the expression are separated in time and space. The closeness or merger of the expression to the essence, is fullness.

Questioner: Could you then almost define time and space as the separation of expression from essence —

Daniel: Time and space is where thought exists. One could say that the identity, or the 'me', is the distance from essence to expression. So that's why full surrender is necessary.

Q: But without that separation through time and space, how would one know, how would one see that it was even necessary to express a quality of God or love?

Daniel: You see, the first 'me' center as identity that we run into is a personal construct. You may experience freedom as far as the personal construct is concerned, so that the feeling and the expression are closer than they have been. But at the same time that you're experiencing that quality, you're also introduced to a subtle conditioning. So that is still a distance between the essence and the expression. At that point, where there is no concentrated personal 'me' structure, there is a great yearning for the essence and the expression to merge. When they move to merge, you'll experience a subtle conditioning — the historical condition, the racial condition.

Q: Is there any other way to see than through this pressure of conditioning?

Daniel: You can't say that seeing isn't taking place; seeing is taking place. But in the moment you also discover that it's not enough, a new awakening takes place.

Q: So that's the movement of life.

Daniel: That's the whole movement. The whole movement of life is that anything removed in time and space from the essence yearns to merge with that essence.

Joseph: Now you are implying that the subtle 'me' has also a resistance of its own that's centuries old, that's not my resistance. What is the force that is going to lead that non-personalized ego to need to come to resolution or to go further?

Daniel: Any time that ego exists as a center, it's always going to clash; there will always be friction there. So we may not have experienced the subtle friction in the past, but once there is not a personalized structure there, you will come to experience the sorrow that exists in form, the sorrow that exists as a collective species. So through friction, through your everyday activity, you come to experience hurt. Now when I say hurt, the hurt is not of the same order as personal hurt — when there was a direct sting, and a response to it. This hurt doesn't leave scars, but this hurt does indicate that there is a greater need.

J: Can we just go back a step here — initially, out of personal hurt, the 'me' is forced to look at itself, and what it's doing; and now that's no longer the case. Can you posit a collective need, or a universal need that is hurting and having to look at itself?

Daniel: No, I come to this: I have recognized that there is an essence in life — that there is some essential quality that can be perceived, first-hand. After experiencing that, I go out into my life, and through one social incident or another, I come to realize that I'm not in touch with that experience any longer. When I realize that I'm not in touch with that quality, a yearning grows in me again to live in that energy all the time. The formulation of that need to live in that energy all the time is merger — is putting merger into action. Each time that I experience that need, receptivity takes place. And at that point I can say discovery has taken place, something has happened. In feeling that, in experiencing that quality, a moment later I again discover its limitation. In discovering its limitation, I again discover that need.

So what is taking place, is that through again and again and again experiencing that need, the gap is being bridged. I come to a point now in life where there is only one need in my life. I have one need, and that need is to live in that quality, to live in that essence — not through any form, not through any idea, because obviously in that journey I have seen the limitation of form, I've seen the limitation of any technique or approach, or any idea system. They're not necessary. But the passion is great, the need is great, and that passion and need is the vehicle. It's sure and it's true.

Now I'm introduced to a life of waiting. Waiting is not inactivity, waiting is not inaction; waiting is a dynamic state. When you have touched and are touched by an essential quality in life, then waiting comes out of recognition; waiting is a dynamic. I would say that true waiting, with understanding that need, with yearning for that quality, is the only real action. You can still be active, you can move around, you can do this, you can do that, you can go from here to there — but everything you do is a conservation of energy. Everything you do is in that grace; everything you do is with that quality. When you experience that there is an essential need in your life to touch the source, then everything that you do expresses that. Without understanding that need and touching that quality in your life, everything you do is a waste of energy, a dissipation of energy.

Questioner: Once there is no more pain, no more conflict in life, how do you know when you're in touch with the energy?

Daniel: You still have signals. Every time the energy is focused — any time you focus energy on any signal, any situation — you've introduced light. Any time you focus your energy on it, you've introduced a quality to that situation that enlightens it. In the glare of that light, what is not real, what is constructed, cannot maintain itself. So you can see if there's a physical disturbance, or a psychological disturbance; and if there is no physical or psychological disturbance, then you've come to the end of the known 'me' — 'me' as a personal construct. Now you may hear sounds, you may hear inner sounds, you may hear the birds, you may hear anything. Whatever calls you, focus your attention on it.

J: The boundaries are wide in that.

Daniel: It's calling you. In focusing your attention on whatever calls you in life, you may be introduced to stillness — a stillness not devoid of feeling, not devoid of sound, not the absence of anything. Stillness, a fertile area — a quality ready to spring into life, a life ready to blossom. In that stillness, the heart speaks. A real dynamic is ready to live.

One Need in Life   167

Questioner: *That is the waiting —*

Daniel: That is the waiting. There's an intensity, a dynamic there, and in that there can be no fear; and the reason that there can be no fear is that there is no space. Fear is the thing that indicates that there is a space between the essence and yourself. When you come to this point of great stillness or waiting in your life, you no longer know what we call psychological fear — there's no psyche as such there. But now you may experience in that stillness, the quality, the connection to all of life; and you may understand why fear and pain are happening in the life around you.

So I can't say that this understanding of the collective pain or sorrow hurts you personally, in the same way that your own psyche hurt you; but you do feel it. It's just not leaving a scar. What's happening now is that when you feel the collective sorrow or pain, you're experiencing a great need in yourself, that's all. So in the past, when you personally felt pain or sorrow, you attempted to run from it. Now, when it's no longer a personal sorrow and pain, but a collective sorrow and pain that you are viewing from the vantage point of your stillness, you feel the connection. And you also see why the sorrow and pain that you see is taking place — it's not a mystery to you.

In that moment, you're experiencing a great need. What you see has introduced you to a further need. And every time that you are introduced to that need, you come closer to an essence. At one point you'll come to understand that there is a need to live in that quality; you'll understand that the reason that it comes and goes, the reason that I've lost sight of it, is because of habit. This coming and going, these moods, ups and downs, these pressures or whatever, are habit — life, death, everything we know is a habit. To understand the need is to live in receptivity. In that stillness, any action that you take is a full action. Because you are aware of the effect; any ill effect indicates that there was some residue in the action, some limit in the action. So, it's not to undo the effect, it's to understand that there's a need for a greater clarification all the time. When you're understanding this need for a greater clarification all the time, you are making a journey in life.

Questioner: Is it a focusing?

Daniel: Focusing is to bring the attention to anything that calls out — not concentrating, but focusing. Concentrating would imply directing the light in such a way that the rest of the vision is in darkness; to me, focusing is an awareness that includes, does not exclude.

Questioner: Includes?

Daniel: Yes, it's able to see, it's able to measure, it's able to feel — it's not separate from what it sees.

Questioner: But actually as you focus on one thing, if you're understanding anything, it must be how this thing is connected to every other thing.

Daniel: Yes. But also in that, while it appears to be everything in terms of your view, a moment later you see that there's some limitation in your view; so your view expands. But at any point, only what you see is what you are. In the next moment you may discover that there was something unseen, you see; you were not that. Only what you see and experience to be yourself is what you are.

You see, if I am limited to my idea of self — as a Christian, as a Jew, or whatever — then obviously the God that I have is the God from my conditioning. That's my view. So then I fit everything into that construct. As I come to understand that this is a limitation, not fulfillment — it's only an extension of myself — then the need to see beyond that becomes great. Just the recognition of that limitation introduces me to a wider view. That wider view looks like vastness — just as the prior view did, you see. So I can't say that one who believes in a God of their conditioning is limited, if they believe in that. But I can say, having an overview of it, that it is limitation, that's all. I can just see the limitation in living according to one's own viewpoint. The viewpoint seems to be one in all, one in everything; but it's only when you come face-to-face with your viewpoint, and you see its limitation, that you're introduced to a wider view — and a wider view, and a wider view.

Now the question was asked earlier, can you ever be sure that the view you have is the widest view? It seems not. And then there is a point where you may see that the stillness is no longer necessary. But before that point, stillness was the all and everything; passion was the immensity, God was the universal. But actually when you're on this journey, you see that they're views. The other evening we discussed the point at which God becomes a limitation. It wasn't a negation, or a perception of God being a limitation, but that the view of God that we would have at any particular time would also introduce us to its limitation — actually it's our limited viewpoint of God that is the limitation. As long as you live in a construct — let's say, of God being the helper — then you're also confined by that, you're also crippled by that.

So then when God is not there, there's room to grow. When God no longer exists as the helper, you're being introduced to true mercy. Because mercy is allowing you to live to your potential, and to experience that you're in fact no longer crippled. Now, the view that you had of God in the past is seen to be a limitation; the need is to grow. Then you're introduced to God as an energy that invites you to go deeper — and as you're able to go deeper, your view expands. The capacity to see is now unending.

4 September 1979

When the Heart Speaks

Allen: It seems that the energy of life doesn't intercede. Someone can carry on for the rest of their days with all sorts of meditative techniques, or adhering to all sorts of forms, and the energy or realization of God or truth will never interrupt and indicate to the person in any way; there is no intercession.

Daniel: But there is, there is intercession. It's not imposing, but it exists. You can see it. We're just busy elsewhere, so we say there's no intercession. We can't see because we're so preoccupied. So it's not as if God or love has no existence; it's because we can't perceive love that it doesn't exist for us. We fill ourselves in with ideas.

A: What does waiting mean?

Daniel: It seems to me that we're bound by our own history, and the collective history of humankind; we're bound to project into the future what we were. That's to be bound in time and space. When you see that, it has a full impact on you. When you actually see that the entire past is what you are and what you will continue to be — see that undiluted, with no capacity to look away, or run away from it — you are introduced to a quality that is no longer bound in that history. So, when I am in this moment aware of the historical process called my past, my present, and my potential future based on that, I see and I feel a great need in my life that I no longer live in repetition. I need to live not artificially, but wholly and fully; I realize that need, and I express that need.

In the expression of that need I'm introduced to what I would call a quality of stillness. There's no longer the chaotic pressure, there is no longer the noise that goes on all the time in the mind which is bound to repeat the past.

In that stillness, waiting can be a fact. Waiting is not therefore waiting *for* something. Because *for* implies space, *for* implies time — some object is coming in the future. But waiting is no longer something bound in the future; waiting is a fact when the being is total, when the total expression is one of yearning, when one understands the need. So waiting is a peace. One comes to peace; there is a total movement of understanding. When you are no longer bound in history, and you express that yearning, you see that the very waiting is the receptivity.

It's difficult, please, move along with it, because the language is limited unless you can perceive it. Waiting appears to be in time, as far as the language is concerned; but the fact is that it's not in time at all. Waiting is God, receptivity is God, merger is God — you're being introduced to different qualities of the same energy. Language is based in time, it's an expression of time; but what is being realized is in fact timeless. Stillness is an introduction, and in the stillness one is introduced further to qualities of light, to qualities of relationship, or love; you see the connection to all the universe. In that, there is no higher or lower. There is no longer a judgmental value; you can see qualities of energy. You may recognize an energy that merges with you; you're just waiting, in that sense, for the merger to take place. When you realize your need, waiting is no problem. It's only a problem to thought, to a thinker who measures waiting in time.

A: So I'm seeing now in simple perception — the mind is quiet, there's no thought taking place per se; but the energy is not moving, it is just kind of gluey or gummed up — that's the only way I can explain it.

Daniel: If there is no movement, it's usually a sign that you're not free to move, that there is a prior call. You may want something more than your capacity to experience it. Most of us want something more than our capacity to actually experience it. So, what we would call non-movement would actually be a saving grace. That non-movement would allow preparation to take place. To those who can't experience the fullness in the moment, then time is utilized. Because sometimes, who can bear this fullness? Who can experience the full understanding, that not only is there no ownership in relationship or possession, but that life, the very life that you call your own, is not your personal possession? So can you bear a real, deep understanding that this life is not something you own, that it's not your personal possession as such?

So we can't see the obvious. And because we can't see the obvious, then we're compelled to feel pain. But the pain is not the problem; the pain in fact indicates, points to an imbalance. But usually we won't see it until there's a crisis.

Questioner: In a state of real stillness and waiting, there is a feeling of fullness. Is fullness the same as stillness?

Daniel: Stillness is a quality that one experiences when they're no longer bound in time, no longer bound in repetition — it's a coming to rest. So stillness is a necessary first step in experiencing something real.

Q: And fullness?

Daniel: Stillness is the quality in which one can take a look and understand directly what they see. The action that comes out of stillness, you can say, introduces one to a quality of fullness — in which everything they do now has some meaning, has some function, is related to a wider picture. One is no longer bound in the past.

Questioner: I really want to experience what you're talking about. And so far, the only thing I know to do is to close my eyes and let my brain just keep going and going; and then I'm expecting that all of a sudden it's just going to stop thinking and I'm going to feel something. Is that what you're talking about?

Daniel: We're talking about something that, essentially, has happened. So what is required is the recognition. It's not something you can force, it's not something that's artificial; it's not that you can push this aside to achieve that. When you do that, what you're actually doing is dealing with a clever mind, which is again ambitious. So what are you left with?

Q: I can't say.

Daniel: But you're left with a quality now — that you're yearning. So that yearning is actually that you've turned on the light, that you've introduced light to whole quality of life. You've introduced light to being a mother, you've introduced light to being a wife. So you're no longer bound in the role, it's no longer a prison; it's a function. And when it is a function, it's sane. Then mind is functioning, it's no longer something that must be changed, or overwhelmed, or overcome, or made to shut up; it's no longer ambitious to survive. It's functioning; it's taking care of what it can take care of. And it recognizes when it cannot take care of something. When it recognizes its limitation, it surrenders, that's all. Then *you* don't have to seek the heart; when mind surrenders to a fact, the heart speaks. It is not that thought is pushed aside or overcome; but to touch the reality, to touch the depth of life, thought is not the correct instrument. The mind surrenders because it's sane, and it realizes its limitation. There is no other way. Any other way, you're not speaking to the heart, you're creating scar tissue. You've made a frightened mind pretend to be heart. You can batter the mind in such a way that it pretends to be divine or holy, but that pretense is only the source of more pain.

When you see the need, you'll also understand what the preparation is. When you experience the need, and there is no merger, it indicates to you that something is still unclear.

So there is nothing wrong with the thinking process. It's just that the entity thinks of itself as the reason for existence, the reason for life, and therefore it's pushing the body around to do this or to have that. It's an opportunistic sort of mentality, constantly looking for an opportunity to continue itself. And so it views life, and everything around it, as opportunity. That opportunity is power, it's continuity, and it's coming out of fear. It could be very simple fears — of loneliness, of being broke and without power, without substance; or the larger fears of being completely disconnected, without a reference point, without a reason; and then the greatest fear, when you see a bit deeper — the actual separation, the separation from love, from God, from contact with anything real. And when there's no contact with anything real, when there's no substance in your life, at that point the mind becomes very active. It's constantly searching to relate itself to something, connect itself to something, acquire some image. It's so frightened without the reference point; it has no existence.

So when one is no longer frightened, when one can no longer experience fear — that psychological drama, that psychological fear — then one has established order in their life. But we want a quality of softness, of stillness, of light, without the order in our social existence, and how can it be? So once I really understand that my need is love, my need is fullness — when I understand that need — I also understand the need for order. So you could say that the heart will only speak fully when the conditions are correct for it to speak, and not before.

Questioner: *Order meaning?*

Daniel: Order meaning whatever it means when you understand the need. There is no book on order. See how chaotic you are, and how divided you are, and what shape this division takes for you. When you see what your fear is, and experience the need, you'll also understand what order means. The basis of traveling is freedom — nothing calls you, nothing has a claim on you; you're free to go. We want love, we want God, we want light, but are we free to experience that? Can you really invite that into your life, can you invite this energy into you fully? And if you invite this quality into your life, then you must have a clean home. If love has any real meaning to you, then you're present, and prepared.

When the Heart Speaks

Questioner: When you say that in stillness, the heart speaks, what do you mean? Does that mean that you feel love? What does it mean when you say that the heart speaks?

Daniel: When there is no competition, and there is no struggle, and there is no going from here to there as a constant — no using the past and projecting the future — when one comes to a quiet, then the action that is expressed is a true action, coming without a motive, coming without continuity. Then the action that comes is not survival-oriented, is not coming out of fear, is not centered. The action that comes from the expression of heart is an action which, although it appears to be individual, is universal. So when the heart speaks, your heart speaks as a channel to the universe. And what happens in the individual when the heart is speaking, is also happening to all life. When the heart speaks, there is no separation. When the mind speaks, there must be separation; it is separation, it's the center. The center always has space outside of it — if I am the center, then you are outside of the center; there's distance between yourself and the rest of life. When the heart speaks, the heart doesn't see the separation. When the heart looks, it sees the connection.

The simple connection can be perceived at a glance. If you have that great intensity, then you'll begin to see more than that. Then your daydreams and ponderings are over, because you're experiencing everything you need to experience in this moment. The fact is where you are, and as you experience the fact where you are, you also experience your connection to all of life. When you experience the connection to all of life, you'll see the energies that apply to you; you'll see the connection. When one experiences the need to touch upon a vastness — when one experiences the need to understand it all, first-hand, clearly and precisely — it must come, it must be. If you recognize what must be, it expresses itself.

12 September 1979

Passages

The following passages have been drawn from larger discussions and interviews.

Questioner: The question about being enlightened, within a certain framework, has come up for me. Can enlightenment exist within the family structure?

Daniel: The family is the very means by which the child is introduced to feeling, to understanding; and through the family the child can also relate to the society, and to life around. But in fact does the family become a habit? It seems that the possibility of freedom or bondage exists in every action.

As an example, you may want to experience love or God, or you may have experienced God, but then it becomes a personalized God — a God of Judaism or a God of Christianity. And then we may go to war with each other over these ideas of God. So now the question is, is it God you're experiencing, or an expanded state of yourself? There may be an initial feeling, but now you've personalized the feeling. And once you've personalized the feeling, you will only use it for your self-perpetuation. So your God now is not God, not love, but something that enhances you, that expands you. So we're talking about a God in our own image, and this God does what we want him to do. And in a similar way, family can become your enclosure, not your introduction.

So the experience of love or family can be an introduction to vastness. But instead, what may take place is that we have the feeling, and then we interpret the feeling, and we cultivate an expression. The expression is self-serving. The God that we've created is now self-serving. The family that we create is self-serving; the country that we're willing to die and live for is self-serving. And when we have a group of self-serving people, we have war. So yes, the expression that may have come out of an original feeling can be the basis of conflict and strife and war. Because the expression is not the fact. God has no name, has no power, cannot be used in any way. Energy does not belong to anyone. Love is not owned by anyone.

* * *

3 July 1979

Daniel: It is only when you understand the nature of the enclosure, the nature of the prison — what the center is, what 'me' is — that you can perceive something deeper than that. Now the only way that one can understand the nature of the enclosure is to yearn to touch something real, to yearn to touch something of essence, without a doubt. Because I see that everything I want and desire and hope for is doubtful; there's a great doubt that it even exists at all, that it has any reality. When the yearning for something real is there and strong, then I look for it everywhere and in everything. That looking is a great need. And when you yearn for that intensity and look with that intensity, there is a response to that very yearning. That response you can call energy or love. Having touched that love, experienced that love — through the yearning I touch the essence called love — a merger takes place. Having experienced that, I now look.

When love looks, it sees love. When essence looks, it sees essence. When light looks, it sees light. Anything that light does at that point has light in it; inherent in each action there is light, there is freedom, there is passion and there is essence. All these words simply mean at this point a direct experience with God — a God that has no name, a God that has no form, a God that belongs to no one, a God that has no power, no influence; but a God that is eternally present, and without which life has no meaning. At that point I come to understand what has been missing in life, and what is missing in this society. Without that experience, without that contact or connection, we are simply going through the motions of life; it is not life itself.

Having experienced it for the moment, my deeper yearning is to live in it totally, to immerse myself in it totally. A part-time God has no meaning now, a part-time experience has no meaning now. When my need is a total feeling, a total living in that intelligent energy, then there must also be an intelligent preparation to allow it to take place. When I yearn for the essence, the essence must respond; it's been waiting, it's been waiting for a human being to yearn, it's been waiting to be recognized. At that point I understand that love waits for a lover. God waits for a full human being.

Questioner: *What's that preparation?*

Daniel: Any time I experience the lack of that love, any time I experience a falling away from that, any time that I experience a resistance or personal desire to continue, there's a direct signal. So the preparation is not some physical act; the preparation is renewed recognition. What is the preparation for eating? It is hunger, a deep hunger. The preparation for a recognition of the essence is a deep passion. And this passion is never satisfied; satisfaction is not a word that applies to passion.

Q: *So the recognition then is really quite a conservation of energy —*

Daniel: Through the act of perception, mutation is taking place. Through the yearning, a transformation is happening. So the preparation is the greater expansion of the very body cells, the very expansion of the brain; the preparation is the capacity of the body to contain the experience. Because the experience is also touching all the limitations, all the conditioning. All the cobwebs are being cleared through it.

So now this journey through light, this journey through essence, touches the source. Through the passion I've experienced a quality that I didn't know existed beforehand. That quality, I come to recognize, is necessary to live. Now I need that, like I need food. I need that like I need water. I need that essence, that essential quality, like I need air to breathe. It's not a choice, it's a great need. Having tasted it, I have a passion for it. That passion is the preparation. The merger with the essence is further preparation. And in the moment I may lose contact with it, that's greater preparation, because my yearning is renewed. Having touched this essence, I am understanding what I am. Through the essence I am introduced to light — a universe as light, a society as light, myself as light — and yet there is deeper to go.

So I come to a point now in this journey where I recognize that there is a source. And without experiencing that source of life directly and clearly and deeply, again life has no meaning. It is a journey without end. It is an eternal voyage that can be described as a blossoming — not a blossoming through time and space, but a continuous blossoming.

***

4 July 1979

Questioner: When I come face to face with people, I seem to want to space out, and I don't like that. I seem to want to run away, and it brings me pain. What's necessary at that point?

Daniel: Pain is simply the message. When you refuse to understand the message, and you run from it, then it chases you. Because then you're trying to run from what you are. In that you may feel more pressure. It's not the pressure that's the problem; it's the attempt to run away from it that's the problem. Because that pain is years of separation, years of isolation. It's the absence of love. That pain is indicating the separation between you and God. That pain is the pain of the fall from grace. That pain is the pain that indicates to you that you replace love, you replace feeling, you replace substance with information and ideas. That pain is indicating to you that your body has never functioned fully. That pain is indicating to you that most of your life is sleep, and it's yearning to wake up. Pain is not something to dismiss; pain is something to be sharp about, to listen to, focus in on.

When you have affection toward that feeling of so-called pain, you transform it. When you look at pain directly and clearly, with all your heart, with all your being, it changes and you change. But all we know now is to run from it. And when you run from it, it's chased you for thousands of years. It can't shut up, it can't keep quiet, you can't get rid of it. It's you — the pain is you. I *am* pain — it's not that I am having pain; the very structure of 'me' is pain, the very structure of 'me' is sorrow. And when I come face to face with that pain or sorrow, I see what I am, and I see what we are. The seeing what I am, is the seeing what we are. The journey begins there.

*   *   *

16 July 1979

Daniel: It's an energy that simply waits. Love is an energy that waits to be recognized. And when that recognition is there, you see yourself through and through. When you yearn for it, when you long for it, when there's nothing else in life for you, when you need to understand it, it's there for you.

Questioner: But a fear is there.

Daniel: No, no; essence won't know fear. What can stop you from it? When your yearning is great enough to understand it, to feel it, nothing will stop you. No one is going to talk me out of that. It's like someone talking me out of breathing. I need to see love. I need to experience it. I need to. So it's the thought of it that creates the fear. Understand the fear, don't run from it.

Q: Something inside says you have to have love, yet the mind tries to confuse the issue.

Daniel: Do you understand why? Because love is death — love is death to the mind. Love is the absence of thought, silence is the absence of this chaotic thought, this choice-maker, the thought process that goes back and forth, that chooses between things. God is not a choice; God is choiceless, love is choiceless. You'll never choose love, you'll always choose your attraction. You'll never choose God, you'll always choose convenience. God and love is not convenient or attractive, it doesn't have these qualities. It's choiceless.

So we're engaged in a very fragile experiment. We're engaged in seeing whether love is possible. Heretofore it hasn't been — or only under certain conditions. And love that only exists under certain conditions, I can't say is an intelligent love any longer. The need is for a love that manifests under all conditions, under all pressures. And the waiting for it will not be painful. Patience is its own reward. That capacity to wait is necessary, and you can only wait when it's clear to you. If you need love — if you need it clearly and precisely, and you understand why — you'll look with that quality.

Q: *There's an empty space that has to be filled.*

Daniel: First recognize the emptiness. The recognition of the emptiness will be the filling. But if you don't understand the emptiness, you'll be haunted.

Q: *What is that emptiness?*

Daniel: That emptiness is 'me'. When I look directly at that emptiness it is transformed. When you look at that emptiness you'll be introduced to light.

Q: *When I do it I feel sadness come up in me.*

Daniel: Don't settle for sadness. Sadness is part of the human condition, but don't get fixed in one role. You're going to see all these clouds, and you're going to see sunshine. Don't get fixed in the sunshine; don't get fixed in the clouds. Then on a rainy day each drop will have loveliness in it, each drop will be a silence. Everything you see, everything you experience, will have silence in it. You don't have to figure out how to go deeper, but just by hearing the rain you'll see how to go deeper. You're just going deeper. You're not asking how to go — you are deeper.

Understand the need — the very formulation of the need is the response. It must come. When you understand it must come, you can wait. It doesn't have a choice if you don't have a choice. If you have a choice, then what you will get will always be limited. So for our further explorations, can we come to this point now of understanding that our need is to see that full flowering, experience that essence, that essential quality. Let's start from that point now — a life without love is not life.

Q: Would you say the work involves no effort?

Daniel: I see that through effort, I can't accomplish it. If I know no other way, then I must make my effort. I am taught effort, in my life I know only effort, and even my attempt to negate effort is still going to be effort. It's still an idea. But when I've exhausted all effort, all known effort, then I still yearn, I still need, but I simply don't know how to go about it any more. And I see at this point that effort tires me out — it's a waste of energy. But the yearning is great.

We must experience yearning without expression. As long as you have expression available to you, you're going to exercise it. But through the futility of expression, you come to a point where you don't know what to do any longer; there's nothing available for you physically to do, you can't accomplish it — and you see it. You come to the point of not knowing what to do; but the yearning is still there. That yearning is an essential quality — yearning without the ability to relieve it, without the ability to run from it, to escape. That point is essential. Before this point the expression was always outward — through activity, through entertainment, through escape of one form or another. Now, when one sees the limitation of the activity, one still needs — very much — but one has nowhere to go and nothing to do. One comes to a crossroad in life. That is the point where one understands the real need.

16 July 1979

* * *

Questioner: *I'm confused about my situation — I don't know what to do. I am planning to go to India to study with this guru, but now it's not clear to me.*

Daniel: Love will wait, the real energy of life will wait — as long as you're not delaying it, and you recognize the fact that you're confused. The recognition of confusion in fact is the preparation for the realization. The confusion, the not knowing, is the only intelligent thing about you at that point. The confusion is very important. Confusion is a quality that allows you to take a rest. When it is no longer confused, and it's clear and precise, then what you do has meaning. But if you push against the confusion, either pro or con, whatever you do is false. You're just moving according to attraction and impulse, you're moving in opposites. And whatever you do in that, you'll suffer a conflict.

So if it's important to you that whatever you do is full and true, then you'll wait until you are full and true. That waiting is really a dynamic. In that waiting, everything you would have gone somewhere else to get, you're receiving. If there is a respect for fullness and truth in you, you haven't lost anything. Can you realize that? Can you realize that just the fact of confusion is your message?

You see, we don't demand of ourselves to have a thinking apparatus that simply contributes pure and clear information. Any time that you have a choice, your action is not pure. Your movement must be really loud and clear and choiceless. Without that level of intelligence or intensity on your part, whatever you do will be lacking — not because it is lacking, but because you're lacking. So confusion is the answer that allows you to take a deep rest.

What you're looking for in life can be realized any time, if you understand what you're looking for.

So let's look at the thoughts we have — because we are enquiring as to what we're after, what do we want? Every time we want something, there's a picture there; so then examine the picture, enquire. What do you want in the ashram? What do you want from this guru? Do you want the robe, do you want the beads, do you want the joining up with the group, do you want a way of life, do you want a philosophy to live by, do you want the security, do you want spiritual blessing, do you want to meet a lover there who thinks the same way you do, do you want to acquire a degree of discipline, do you want to antagonize your parents? You see, we are a product of our society, and these things are also important to everyone in the society — security, fear of being alone, being someone, having a guideline or discipline to live by, antagonizing our parents as a way of escaping from their rule, a desire for them to love you — all these things we are. The society, and most of us, are conditioned to feel a certain way, and we do experience it in our life. When you have no money in your pocket you know fear. When there's no one in bed with you, you may know loneliness. When you see that you're getting on in age and you can project that there's no one with you, there can be great fear that no one will care for you when you're older. When you're having children, or you don't have children, you may know fear.

Q: I do have a sense of what I'm looking for, and I realize that I'm looking for something outside of me to give me unconditional love — and that's what makes me stuck. Somewhere inside me, I don't know about that any more.

Daniel: It's very important that I am not seeking what I call unconditional love as a reaction to my failure in romance. That is not unconditional love. As long as you are looking for love, and it's involved in human form, the human form always has a condition. When you have a condition, then what you find also has a condition. So how can you find more than you are? The arrangements you've made in your life reflect you — reflect your moods, reflect your anxieties, reflect your fears. So if you've wanted someone to give you a sense of security, you've only required or desired a sense of security because you felt insecure. We move in a sort of opposite; in our weakness we're looking for a strength. Strength is not unconditional love. So even in that phrase, unconditional love, there's a condition imposed. What picture do you have of unconditional love? Stay with it please, if you can — because it's really an important time. What do you really want in this life — can you see it clearly?

Q: *Well, I would like to be more at peace. There's a lot of war inside me; lately there has been so much up and down — and I would like that to change.*

Daniel: Is that all you want, then? More peace, or peace?

Q: *Peace.*

Daniel: Why can't you have that? If it exists, why can't you experience it?

Q: *I don't allow myself to have it actually.*

Daniel: Okay, so please understand it. Then your talk of peace is only a reaction to the war that's going on inside of you. The most that you can accomplish with your effort is truce. And truce will only come when you create one dominating force inside of you that can shout down the others. And if you can adopt a philosophy that tells you what is right, you'll be able to shout down these other forces. But the war will continue in a subtle way. So if you need peace actually, then understand the many ways that you make war with yourself. Just understand it — don't overcome it, just understand it. My feeling is that life has quality; there's vastness to be realized — and that from this moment on, whatever the pressure on you, you still must treat this life with a feeling of preciousness. And if you are intent on experiencing truth in your life

— so that you can say yes, this is true — that must come about. You're not that far removed from it. Wait for it with intensity.

* * *

16 August 1979

Questioner: I have a very down-to-earth question. I have a two-and-a-half year old little boy, and I'm in a position of having to exert an influence on his life. And we inevitably have conflicts, and I really don't know how to deal with it. I don't want to destroy him, I don't want to project on him, I don't want to impose myself, but at the same time he has to be somebody he feels good about — living in the world, with his mother and his father; and we have to feel good about him. I really don't know how to deal with the situation. I hate to use the word discipline, I don't believe it, I don't know what that is. But, how do you help a little person grow up?

Daniel: What do you need in life?

Q: I feel that I need freedom from suffering, and a sense of joy in every moment.

Daniel: Do you need it thoroughly?

Q: I think so — yes.

Daniel: If you understand that need, you won't create any difficulties, any further difficulties in your life. If you understand that need, then what you do will facilitate that understanding. If you need that, obviously the child needs that. If you experience that in your life, there will also be room for those around you to experience it. If you don't experience that in your life, then how can you provide it?

Q: Well, until I experience it, how can I avoid destroying him?

Daniel: You see, it's not an 'until'. If there is a need for you to experience full freedom in your life, then you also must provide that basis for him. You'll have to see the difference between mother and Mommy; between response and performance on your part. You'll have to see the difference between responding to the youngster's need, and playing Mommy and getting feedback from the youngster. And yet you'll still have to care — as long as there's a physical need, you'll have to provide that. But you'll also have to see, in that provision, not to create bondage. Just the very feeling of the need for freedom will mean that there's freedom in the action — you'll be providing it with that concern. And even if you've make a mistake, there will be a moment where you can clarify it. Try not to rely on apology, try not to rely on excuses. In other words, when you don't have any formulas available to you, then you'll make sure that each movement is as essential as it can be. Make mistakes — what's the harm — but experience the love. The mistakes will pass in time; through the mistakes you'll come to understand mechanically what's the right thing. But if you're in touch with that essential quality, if you're in touch with that need for freedom in yourself, you'll provide that also. So there is a connection there. To understand that connection is to provide.

You know, we've relied on experts to such an extent that we've lost touch with even knowing what to eat. According to the experts, we need this much protein, that much vitamin — it's all idea. We don't even experience a full hunger any more. We are the only beings on this planet that have to figure out their diet — and however closely you figure it out, it always seems to come up short. And now we have to figure out our relationship to the youngster, and how to provide. But at the same time that you're doing that figuring out, can you also understand the need for this quality to awaken in you again? We were discussing this the other day in the case of health. At the same time that I'm taking medicine for my illness, I also see the need not to have to take medicine, not to be dependent on this form. At the same time I'm jogging to be healthy, can I also understand the need that health is not won by these things? Because if I'm depending on the jogging,

I can't be healthy. I can still do the jogging, but let me understand that the only real jogging is in enjoying, not in the program. I understand that the only real eating is in hunger, real hunger — there's a vital quality there. When I'm eating according to time or ritual, then I may be bound by that known, or that information.

But can I understand the need to be free? Let's try it — it would be a lovely experiment if through the child we could understand the need for freedom in the family, in the relationship. If you understand the need for freedom or fullness, or a full experience of life in yourself, then you must also understand the need for freedom in every human being. You may not be able to create that condition for every human being, but you can realize the need for it. So at least you won't add to the burden. You may not create freedom for others, but you won't create sorrow. That would be fine enough — that there's one human being somewhere who's not creating any more damage. That to me is the essential first step in helping, that you're not hurting anything — not that you're helping anything, but that you're one human being, one person who is not going to hurt knowingly.

So I can provide you with a formula, but if you can see the basic need, it will occur to you how to move. If you can see the basic need that you have to experience freedom, or this softness, then the child in your charge also needs to experience that; that will allow for a soft quality.

My premise is that two beings that are fully in love, in intelligent love — a love that is tested, a love that is examined and understood — must in their merger produce clarity. Because when people are making love — engaging in physical lovemaking without fantasy, without projection, without thinking of climax or anything like that, are just engaged in loving each other, they simply merge — the product of that love to me is pure, is without prior conditioning. That to me would be what the Virgin birth means; it's the quality of innocence. The quality of innocence at that point for Mary was that it was the Lord's child, not her own. It was a child that was not made by man. So, at that point the parents entered into a relationship with the child that was without imposed conditions; they were simply guardians to the child. They were a family of beings who lived together, who were growing together.

So the act of motherhood is not an imposed condition; it is really a response. You could say that mother and child is a vibration, a merger — they're energies that merge. And relationship, real relationship only takes place when you come to understand the qualities of energy — and you see what fits.

Q: I see.

Daniel: Realize your need and you'll also realize the youngster's need. If it's difficult at times, if you can remember, leave the child alone a bit. And also, try not to give him too many toys. Let him have a few minutes of quiet without something to do all the time. We're always giving the children something to do — always giving them a crayon or a coloring book, or picking them up and throwing them around. Or you may say "You're the father, play with him", or something like that, and then the father may feel compelled to play with the child, even if he doesn't feel like it. The child knows when it's artificial, when you're playing Poppa or playing Momma. So you can refrain from that performance. Because what you're doing now is engaging in a delicate experiment; great care and affection is necessary. When there's no authority to refer to, then you must find this quality in yourself.

29 August 1979

* * *

Questioner: I still find that I have this need to pray.

Daniel: What do you pray for?

Q: To feel fuller in my life.

Daniel: And so have you asked for that — not fuller, but fullest — can you ask for the fullest?

Q: *I don't know what the fullest is.*

Daniel: But you know fuller. And you know that fuller is in time — a bit more. Why not go now as far as prayer can carry you? Prayer was a tool that existed for someone who needed it, you see. But prayer past a certain point becomes a limit, bondage, a burden.

Q: *You mean it becomes habit.*

Daniel: Yes; it becomes habit, because you've established an association with an energy called God only in a way of help. You've established, then, a relationship of help; even though you may not need help any longer, you may have associated a relationship with God where you're constantly seeking help from this energy. It would be my feeling that we need to come to a point in life where we can walk together with this energy, and in fact experience and express this quality in our daily life. Then prayer will have a different quality. Prayer is in your eating, prayer is in your walking, prayer is in your sitting, prayer is in the way you hold your body — prayer is in the way you're living. So now you can't say that there is a moment called prayer; prayer is life, it's an offering. But when you identify with one expression, you've also limited yourself by that. So to me it's not a negation of prayer; but now we come to a point of expansion of prayer, in which one takes full human responsibility. I needed help, and I prayed.

Q: *And it's been answered.*

Daniel: The prayers have been answered all year, and there's still a question. What's the question now? Have you felt the need to be that quality you pray to?

Q: *I have.*

Daniel: Now the need is to live a life of prayer — not prayer that wants, but prayer that needs to experience that very quality, that needs to live that very quality, that needs to be that very quality.

To me, we must now be introduced to an intelligence that no longer has this separation between itself and this energy that it needs. That's what I meant before about the journey to the source. Any time that you're no longer imposing a condition, there's always a movement to the source of energy, to the essence. Form is removed from essence; and given the opportunity, form will always move to the essence; and in moving to the essence it transforms, it changes. As you approach that quality that you pray to, something is changing also in your life, in your form, in your very being. But we tend to get stuck in a form. We tend to get stuck at a distance. When one gets stuck, a great need comes. At that moment, to recognize the need is the movement again. That being stuck generates a great need, a great yearning again. That yearning is the movement. So it's not a negation of prayer, it's just now a need to be that very quality we pray to.

Q: I feel this need to surrender — you've spoken about this quality of surrender. I find that when I'm able to surrender, a fullness seems to enter. I find this quality difficult. In my daily life — we've spoken about bringing this quality into one's daily life — I find that, in conducting business, or in other situations, I just find it difficult to surrender.

Daniel: Surrender is not some option, or some act of volition. You can't artificially create the structure of surrender. But what you can do is recognize the need to love. So you need to experience this quality, this essence wherever you are; recognize the need wherever you are. A mind that seeks to surrender is a mind that thinks that it has something to let go of. Surrender is the recognition that you have nothing. So a being who understands the need, really, has also put the response in motion.

2 September 1979

* * *

Questioner: What is truth?

Daniel: Truth is an expression of essence; it is the changing expression of an unchanging quality. And one who touches that essence fully lives in truth.

8 September 1979

* * *

Questioner: If we are engaged in thought, can we actually participate in anything real?

Daniel: The energy that waits, waits to be recognized. The recognition takes place only when thought sees its limitation and surrenders.

Q: So thinking is a dissipation of the energy?

Daniel: Thinking is a process that does not allow one to see a fact, the fact of life. When thought realizes its limitation, the mere seeing of the limitation is an act of surrender.

Q: It seems that there's a choice — either thought or . . .

Daniel: Or further thought. There is a choice between qualities of thought; but there is not a choice in reality. Reality can't be a choice. You can choose between this shirt or that shirt, this house or that house; this religion or that religion, there you can exercise your choice. But there's no choice in love, and there's no choice in God. There is choice of gods, there is choice of lovers — but no choice in actual love.

29 September 1979

* * *

Questioner: What is a guru — or is a guru necessary?

Daniel: When one realizes the need to love fully and purely, you can say that this realization is the heart speaking. When one realizes the need to love, when one yearns to love, there is a response to that need. The response to that need, to me, would be called guru. So to me, guru means that I see my heart in front of me. What I see, when I see you, is my heart. In seeing you, I'm introduced to my heart; the qualities are the same.

When one touches that quality in life, the question whether there should or shouldn't be a guru seems to be without any meaning. The question is not should there be a guru, or shouldn't there be a guru; the question is, do I need love in my life? To me, the answer is yes. What form it takes, what the response will be — that is not my question. My question is, is it true, is it real? Is it a response that I can perceive to be eternal, and vast? When one realizes the need to love, the manifestation of that realization I would call the guru. The guru is not something you seek; guru is a response to your awakening, to your need, to your yearning.

Q: A guru is not something you need?

Daniel: Guru is not something you seek. When you seek a guru, what you're seeking is coming from your thought, so what you find will be your projection. But when there is a response that comes out of pure yearning, a pure realization of the need, that response is a reflection of your heart, your essence. Seeking is an intellectual exercise; yearning is a quality of the heart, an opening of the heart. And the true guru is a response to this yearning.

30 September 1979

III. REFLECTIONS
Writings from the Author's Journal

Yearning

Throughout recorded religious history we can see a quality of yearning — the ancient Hebrews for God and Messiah; in yogic texts the yearning of the female aspect Shakti for her lord Shiva; in the religious poetry of Kabir, who likens himself to the bride yearning for God the groom; in the passionate songs of Mirabai for her Lord Krishna — in short, yearning or longing — or we may say passion — seemed to be a necessary expression if one were to realize fulfillment.

12 *July 1979*

* * *

Deeper Enquiry

As the enquiry deepens, one is introduced to the many subtle forms of conditioning — the pursuit of pleasure, of personal survival, the center of the universe being 'me'. And with that center one attempts to impose oneself on life. Seeing the utter shallowness of this self-centered existence, one becomes aware of the collective conditioning — an attempt to give oneself meaning through a cause or philosophy, an attempt to expand the 'me' center which is now 'we'. And now this 'we' attempts to impose its views and ideas on the life around it. Seeing the mediocrity and futility of a life fixed on 'me' or 'we', one enquires deeper.

in that stillness . . .

At this point in the enquiry, one needs a great intensity, because we are leaving behind the false security of tradition and recorded history, and approaching a life without fixed reference points.

Now one can see that mankind has attempted, through tradition and philosophies, through nations and language, through his activities, to provide a sense of security and meaning for himself — a sense of purpose — and repeatedly it has collapsed. We come to a point in our enquiry when we recognize that nothing we invent or create through our ideas will provide what we need. And yet we still yearn, we still need, and nothing that we can obtain through effort can relieve our yearning. That yearning is the passion, is the quality necessary for the further journey into life. When we yearn, we awaken a response. The response will always be gauged by the quality of our yearning. Love is the response when one yearns deeply — essence is the response to passion — God is a response to a full human being. When essence merges with passion, when a human being merges with God — a birth takes place.

25 July 1979

* * *

Need

Without an understanding of the actual need, the capacity to realize it is not possible. Understanding the need creates the receptivity — which in turn is an invitation for this energy to enter. Receptivity — a marriage, a journey in stillness.

14 August 1979

* * *

Awakening

One finds oneself confined in history.
One sees in an incident the act of repetition, the same thing over and over, and one experiences all of the past in that moment. One sees that one is the result of the past, the personal past, as well as the result of the entire history of humankind. Seeing that, one views the future and sees the future also as the extension of that same history, with some modifications. Seeing the continuity, seeing the repetition, seeing the all of it in the moment — to see it totally is to be introduced to a great need — a yearning for newness, freshness, something real, not bound by history and time. To realize the need is the receptivity necessary — in that receptivity or stillness love can flower.

29 August 1979

* * *

Essence

Having touched this essential energy, the journey begins — a journey not bound in time or space; a flowering — one realizes the great need to see and experience the essence always —
The very merger in essence transforms and is transforming — life is now a dynamic — the simplest chores and movements — walking, eating, working, sitting — are now movements without friction. Seeing the essence in everything, seeing the qualities of energy, one moves in a dance of harmony with all of life.

1 September 1979

* * *

Health

Experiencing stillness, one also touches upon a quality of life that is without friction — a softness and affection is felt for all of life — an experience of affection inwardly and outwardly. This affection works its magic, allowing the body to soften and realize one's potential. This then is health — a health not dependent on potions and activity, but a dynamic life of realized potential. Through our past activities we have imposed a condition upon ourselves. This imposed condition of psychological conflict, where the thoughts lead one to live a life out of balance, is illness. When stillness enters, the balance is restored — then and only then is the body fit enough to participate in this journey. Flexible enough to adapt and respond, we may touch upon a life no longer subject to illness and stress — this vastness, or a life without limits — this is the actual basis of health.

* * *

14 September 1979

Light

When one sees the limitation of a self-centered existence, activities and pressures cease, and a stillness is experienced. In that stillness, one can see the light at the end of the tunnel. A great yearning to merge and live in that light takes place — life's journey, to live in the light — to see that light, to feel it, to live it. All formerly mundane activity now is a movement of light, and through these simple everyday actions one experiences a life no longer bound in fear, but a life of light — to merge with that light is called surrender — one has discovered full meaning and purpose without effort or stress.

* * *

17 September 1979

Community

When one awakens to the need for love to flower, one also sees the need for that quality to awaken in all humanity. This then is community — an understanding of the mutual need to touch fullness and light.

22 September 1979